THE M.C.C. CRICKET COACHING BOOK

Gary Sobers. Power and perfection *Patrick Eagar*

THE M.C.C.
CRICKET COACHING
BOOK

Published officially for
The M.C.C. by
THE KINGSWOOD PRESS

The Kingswood Press
an imprint of William Heinemann Ltd
10 Upper Grosvenor Street, London W1X 9PA

LONDON MELBOURNE
JOHANNESBURG AUCKLAND

First published by Naldrett Press Ltd
April 1952
Reprinted 1952, 1954

Second edition published by the Naldrett Press Ltd
in association with the World's Work (1913) Ltd 1955
Reprinted 1957, 1959

Third edition published by William Heinemann Ltd 1962
Reprinted 1965, 1968, 1972, 1974

Fourth edition published by William Heinemann Ltd 1976
Reprinted 1980

Fifth edition published 1987

0 434 98080 3 /3

Printed in Great Britain by Redwood Burn Ltd, Trowbridge
and bound by WBC Ltd, Maesteg

BUCKINGHAM PALACE.

I once heard someone quote Oscar Wilde as having said that 'if a thing is worth doing it is worth doing badly'. There is a grain of truth in it but it misses the far more important point that the better you can do something the more pleasure you get out of it.

There are, of course, 'naturals' in all games. They seem to know by instinct how to cope with any situation in a flash. They appear to have an inborn sense of timing and balance which allows them to defy the normal rules although this originality is the despair of purists and coaches. But these fortunate players are the exceptions; ordinary mortals need to combine what natural talents they have with a good proportion of coaching and an even larger proportion of practice.

Coaching itself is quite an art and often unrelated to brilliance in the game. Just as some have a natural genius for cricket so there are coaches with a special flair for giving instruction and encouragement and for stirring up enthusiasm. The rest need all the help they can get.

The M.C.C. Cricket Coaching Book sets out to give just that help by drawing on the experience and methods of leading players and coaches. With advice anyone with an enthusiasm for cricket can become a useful coach and any ambitious player can improve his performance in all departments of the game.

PRESIDENT OF M.C.C.
1949–50 AND 1974–5

Contents

For their assistance in providing photographs for this edition the M.C.C. and publishers wish to thank Patrick Eagar; Adrian Murrell, Michael King and Simon Bruty of All-Sport; The Photo Source; The Press Association; and Mr J. G. Dunbar.

The drawings for this edition are the work of Bruce Drysdale, Harry Bloom and David Merryweather.

Preface

The formation of the M.C.C. Youth Cricket Association and the introduction of a Coaching Award Scheme in January 1952 were important steps in the development of cricket in the U.K. These events had fortunately been anticipated and a new and detailed book on the basic skills of the game was well advanced.

The first edition of *The M.C.C. Cricket Coaching Book* was published late in 1952 and in the foreword to that book the then President of M.C.C., Mr W. Findlay, said it represented the first official attempt by the Club to review the whole field of the game's technique. Since then there have been two revised editions and eight reprints, and well over 60,000 copies have been sold throughout the world. Before the publication of each edition many conferences and coaching courses were held at the Lilleshall National Sports Centre and the opinions of distinguished players and coaches were sought.

In the 1962 edition Mr H. S. Altham, in his foreword, wrote 'Though the first object of this book is to suggest to the coach what to teach and how to teach it, it is hoped that it may also appeal to the young cricketer who is keen to know what to learn and how to apply it, and even perhaps to the more mature player who may be reminded by it of things he has forgotten or find old truths presented, perhaps, in a fresh light.'

In 1967 the National Cricket Association took over the responsibility for the development of the National Coaching Scheme. As a result of their experience in this field they decided, early in 1974, to set up a working party to appraise the situation and, if it was thought that the book required revision, to seek M.C.C.'s approval and collaboration.

Since the book was first published in 1952, progress in techniques, visual aids and teaching methods have changed and contributed greatly to higher standards in sport. Cricket has been no exception and a number of changes and innovations have already been adopted. In the field of coaching, for example, the syllabus of the Advanced Course has been considerably extended; national and staff coaches have been appointed; a Teachers' Award has been introduced, intended primarily for Students in Colleges of Education; five new instructional films have been produced, and a Proficiency Awards Scheme for boys and girls introduced.

In light of these developments and the knowledge gained from them, the working party concluded that, whilst the philosophy and aims of the book should remain – a tribute indeed to the late Mr H. S. Altham and his two co-authors, Mr G. O. Allen and Mr H. P. Crabtree – some revision of the text and illustrations was now required. Four additional chapters dealing with N.C.A. Proficiency Awards Scheme, Fitness for Cricket, Non-Turf Pitches and The Laws have been added. The working party consisted of G. O. Allen, H. P. Crabtree, J. T. Ikin, A. S. M. Oakman, R. Morris and the three National Coaches, K. V. Andrew, R. G. M. Carter and L. J. Lenham. P. W. Sutcliffe also helped in the early stages of the revision of the 4th edition of the book.

In 1986 a further revision was undertaken to produce this 5th edition. The photographs and layout were revised by Sir George (G. O.) Allen, Lt. Col. J. R. Stephenson (Acting Secretary, M.C.C.), D. Wilson (M.C.C. Head Coach), and K. V. Andrew (NCA Director of Coaching).

The grateful thanks of the M.C.C. and the N.C.A. are due to them and others who have so willingly given their time and contributed their wide experience to the production of this edition of *The M.C.C. Cricket Coaching Book*.

1

The Spirit of the Game

Cricket is, in a sense, warfare in miniature and a cricket match should be fought out by both sides with all the resources of spirit and technique at their command. At the same time it should always be a recreation, a game to be played not only according to written laws but in harmony with an unwritten code of chivalry and good temper.

A cricket team should feel that they are playing with, as well as against, their opponents. The home side should remember that they are hosts, the visitors that they are guests, and both should realize that the true greatness of the game lies in combat and comradeship combined.

Pursued in such a spirit, victory, and nothing short of victory, should be the object of both teams from the first over of the match. The bowlers and fielders of the one, the batsmen of the other, should go on to the field determined to attack and to go on attacking until they are really forced to fall back on defence, and even then to resume the offensive directly the balance of the game permits.

It would seem that of recent years this instinct for attack has tended to give place to a premature concern with defence in which the batsman's chief aim is to stay at the wicket rather than to make runs and the bowler's is to keep down the rate of run-getting rather than to get wickets. With the resulting development of defensive technique in batting, bowling and field-placing, the game is in danger of becoming less vital and less enjoyable for players and spectators alike.

The coaches of today can do cricket no greater service than by helping the cricketers of the future to engender the spirit and the armoury of attack: only so can they win from the game the best that it has to give them.

In no other game perhaps are the individual and his team so closely integrated. One man can virtually win a match, not necessarily by technical skill, but by intelligence, concentration and character: one man can lose it by a failure in those qualities. Conversely the morale of each member of an eleven can be largely built up and sustained by the atmosphere of the whole. Unity of purpose and belief in each other is a tremendous asset in cricket, and it is usually possible to sense it by watching a team take the field or listening to them talk as they sit and watch the game from the pavilion.

Nor does any other game expose a player to a more varied or exacting trial. It can be a lonely and formidable experience to walk out, perhaps after a long wait, to bat at the crisis of a match, possibly to face a fast bowler on a lively pitch, or a spinner on a turning one: formidable too to stand under a high catch knowing that to miss it may cost the game. Bowler and fielder alike may often towards the end of a hard day have to 'steel their hearts' for a final effort.

There are also the less obvious but more insidious trials of failure and success: the greatest players will have spells when nothing will go right; then comes the test of still keeping cheerful and finding some consolation in the success of others: and if fortune smiles for a time and the game seems easy, the true cricketer will remember to keep a modest mind.

2

Fielding

The better fielding side is usually the one which wins the match. **No one who is not prepared to do his best to become a good fielder has the right to call himself a cricketer.** For as fielder, more even than as batsman or bowler, he is a member of a team and can not only determine the result of a game by a catch, a run out or a saved boundary, but, as long as he is on the field, can inspire or depress his team mates by example. Nothing reveals more clearly the spirit of a team, the leadership of its captain and the inspiration of its coach than the quality of that team's fielding: moreover, fine fielding not only constitutes an immense reinforcement to its bowlers, but presents to the opposing batsmen a formidable front, psychological as well as physical. At the very highest level of cricket the standard of fielding, particularly close catching and throwing, has never been better than at the present time. **Perhaps the most important of all cricket truths which a coach can instil is that fielding is fun, and infinitely more fun if everyone tries.**

THE BASIC PRINCIPLES

There is no reason why any team should field badly provided they are keen enough and their practice is wisely and enthusiastically directed. Of course people differ widely in their physical gifts and what is easy and natural to one person may only be achieved by long and determined practice by another. Good fielding calls for quick starting, quick stooping and balance. These can be stimulated by exercises in a gymnasium, but the major part of the job has to be done outside and with a ball.

The modern game demands that each player has good all-round fielding ability. Although a fielder may specialize in one or two positions, he must be competent to field anywhere and especially away from the wicket he must be able to collect and return the ball quickly and accurately from the outfield.

Good fielding also means good backing-up: wherever a player may be fielding he must be ready to position himself well behind one wicket or the other so that returns from fieldsmen do not result in overthrows: few things demoralize a team more quickly than runs given away unnecessarily.

Later in this chapter the technique of fielding in each position is described, but no player can afford to heed only one section.

N.B. Everything that follows is written for a right-arm thrower: for a left-armer reverse 'left' and 'right'.

Stopping and returning

As the bowler reaches the crease, all except the close fieldsmen will be moving in towards the batsman. Whilst the mental attitude of fieldsmen must be aggressive, their first job is to stop the ball, as only then can they attempt to return it quickly and accurately. To stop a ball a fielder must

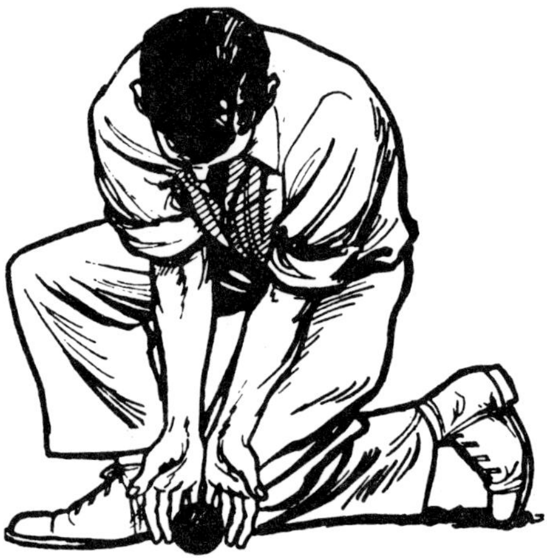

Fig. 1. Stopping: the long barrier position: right foot, with left knee overlapping, at right-angles to line of ball: head directly over hands

first get to it, and this means being able to start directly he has sighted the line of the stroke. To start quickly he must:

1. **Watch the batsman** so as to anticipate the likely line of the stroke.
2. **Be balanced** with the body slightly stooped and with the hands hanging loosely at the ready in front of him.
3. **Concentrate,** expecting each ball to be hit to him.

To stop the ball he must:

1. **Get on to the line of the ball** as quickly as possible.
2. **Get down early and stay down.**
3. **Keep the head still,** watching the ball until it is safely in his hands.

The best position for receiving the ball, especially one that has been firmly struck, is called the LONG BARRIER position (Fig. 1).

For a ball to his right, the fieldsman moves on to the line of the ball

Fig. 2.
Throwing:
poised with the eyes looking along the left arm, which points straight at the target: weight just beginning to be transferred to the left foot

Fig. 3. Throwing: the follow-through: full pivot, led by head and right arm, straight down the line of the ball

and turns his right leg and foot sideways to it, dropping on to his left knee which will just overlap the right heel: his body will thus present the maximum barrier to the ball. His hands will be down to receive the ball in front of the left knee, fingers pointing to the ground, little fingers touching. His head will be directly over his hands and in line with the ball so that he can watch it into his hands with both eyes level. From this position he can step forward with his left leg into the throwing position.

For a ball to his left, if there is not time to adopt the procedure described above, he will drop on his right knee just overlapping the left foot. He will now pivot on his right foot so that he can step forward into the throwing position.

Throwing

Fast and accurate throwing is essential for aggressive fielding. It will make the most of any chance of running a batsman out and will slow down the rate of scoring. Though really fine throwing demands special flexibility and strength, anyone can learn to throw adequately, with speed and accuracy. The chief points in throwing techniques are:

1. The right foot starts at right-angles to the intended line of throw, with the knee bent and the weight fully on this foot.
2. As the left foot steps towards the target, so the throwing arm, with elbow bent and wrist cocked, should travel on a line straight back from the shoulder. At the same time the front arm and hand stretch out to point at the target (Fig. 2).
3. The head must remain level – eyes looking at the target.
4. As the weight is transferred on to the front leg, so this leg straightens and twists to thrust the body towards the target.
5. The throwing arm should strike as late as possible so that at the moment of release of the ball the chest is facing the target.
6. The action of the front leg and throwing arm continue, forcing the body into the follow-through: the head now looks at the target over the throwing shoulder, which points at the target (Fig. 3).

For sheer speed of return, especially over short distances, the throw from below the shoulder can be very effective, but it is more difficult to control for length and direction. Coaches will be wise to stick to the safer technique in which the throwing arm travels along a vertical plane; however, all fielders should be encouraged to experiment and practise other techniques, once the safe method has been mastered.

From short distances a fast underhand return may be the most effective. The ball should be gathered when the left leg is leading and the hand is level with the foot: the head must be kept down until the ball is safely in the hand. Since the pick-up is made with one hand and the fieldsman is moving at full speed this method of return requires constant practice.

David Gower. Concentration and mobility, not to mention bravery, are needed to make catches like this *All-Sport/Adrian Murrell*

Clive Lloyd, a great fielder in any position: here in the slips he has a good base, and his eyes closely watch the ball right into his hands *All-Sport/Adrian Murrell*

Headingley, 1975. The England close fielders get down and keep down, 'hoping for the kill' *Patrick Eagar*

Intercepting and returning

In this technique the object is to gather the ball in such a position that the throw can follow immediately, indeed can almost be regarded as part of a single process. For this skill the fielder must:

1. **Intercept the line of the ball as quickly as possible:** this means not only on to it but in to it.
2. If he has time, turn sideways in the last stride with the right foot landing at right-angles to the line (Fig. 4).
3. **Bend both hips and knees so that the ball is received in both hands just in front of the right foot** and with the weight of the body on that foot with the fingers pointing to the ground (Fig. 5).
4. **Get the head in line with the ball:** the eyes remain fixed on the ball until it is in the hands.
5. From this position, **step forward with the left leg into the throwing position.**

Chasing and returning

(*a*) *Over a short distance:*

Often the speed of the ball will beat the fielder and he must turn and chase it before being able to make his return. Time is often lost by an inefficient pick-up: a vital fraction of a second can mean the difference between a safe run and a run-out.

The important points are:

1. The fielder must pursue the ball as fast as possible.
2. The fielder who throws right-handed must chase the ball so that it is on his right-hand side.
3. As he stoops to pick up the ball he should bend down low so as not to over-balance.
4. The pick-up is off the right foot.
5. From this position the body pivots to face the wicket and is immediately in the throwing position.

(*b*) *Over a long distance:*

Because the distance to be thrown is greater the fielder must be able to get more body weight into the throw. The technique is the same as for short distance except that:

1. As he steps into the pick-up his last stride should be as long as possible without over-balancing.
2. The pick-up is off the left foot instead of the right.

Fig. 4.
Intercepting:
the body in an accelerated approach has turned sideways, with the right foot in the final stride landing at right-angles to the line of the ball

Fig. 5.
Intercepting:
the hands are down to receive the ball just in front of the right foot: head and eyes directly above point of interception

3. As he pivots, he steps towards the target with the left foot: this allows the whole body to come into the throwing position.

N.B. When chasing a ball which is travelling near to the fielder's maximum running speed, the fielder will not be able to pick up without some degree of overbalance. Gifted fielders, with a 'strong arm' will be able to throw in an 'off balance position', and they should be encouraged to develop their own style. The majority of players, and especially young players, should be encouraged to return the ball using the technique described, whenever possible.

Catching

(*a*) *Away from the wicket:*

Quite as many catches are missed by faulty positioning, or by lack of balance, as by any failure of the hands to grip the ball. The essentials of safe catching are:

1. **Do not move until the flight of the ball has been judged.**
2. Get on to the line quickly.
3. **Keep the head still and watch the ball all the way.**
4. Make a wide but relaxed target for the ball with the hands and fingers: the ideal place to catch the ball is at the base of the fingers which should automatically close round it (Fig. 6).
5. **Make the catch at eye level, letting the hands and arms give naturally with the ball:** the catch will be completed in front of the chest.

If the ball is travelling along a flatter trajectory, but still arriving at head height, it will be necessary to modify this technique:

1. The palms of the hands, slightly cupped, should be facing the line of the ball.
2. Make a wide, but relaxed, target with the fingers pointing upwards and the thumbs touching.
3. The catch should be completed just to one side of the head: the hands and arms will ride naturally with the ball (Fig. 7).

(*b*) *Close to the wicket:*

In recent years close-to-the-wicket fielding has become increasingly specialized and the techniques demand a good deal of practice and experience. Qualifications necessary for a close fielder are quick reactions and an ability to concentrate. In order to react quickly it is essential to have the correct stance:

1. **The weight should be evenly distributed and balanced between both feet,** which are comfortably apart, about shoulder width, or slightly more.
2. The knees should be bent and the seat well down, with the weight of the

body on the balls of the feet, so that the fielder can push forwards or sideways off either foot.

3. The hands should be forward and ready to receive the ball, **fingers pointing down and palms towards its likely direction.**

Fig. 6. Catching a high ball: head steady and eyes on the line: fingers well spread: the ball will be caught at about eye level

Fig. 7. Catching a ball of flat trajectory: palms of hands facing the line of the ball

4. The head should be still and the eyes level (Fig. 8).
5. Close-in fielders tend to rise too early. **A golden rule is 'get down and keep down'.** Do not move until the ball has been sighted off the bat. Fielders should get down as the bowler approaches the crease.
6. The ball should be watched into the hands, but the hands must be relaxed to 'give' with the ball to prevent it from bouncing out.

Fig. 8. Close to the wicket: body well down and balanced: fingers relaxed and pointing down: head still

FIELDSMEN AWAY FROM THE WICKET

The chief qualifications for these fieldsmen are:

(*a*) Pace to convert possible twos into ones, and to cut off boundaries.

(*b*) A powerful and accurate throw.

A fieldsman away from the wicket will find the following considerations helpful:

1. **He should always be moving in as the ball is bowled,** watching first the ball and then the batsman. Observation and experience will often enable him to anticipate the direction of the stroke and so get a valuable start to intercept the ball.
2. On sighting a high hit he should not immediately rush in, but should **wait until he has been able to judge the length and line of the ball accurately.** Once he has done this the sooner he can get into position for a catch, and the more balanced and still he can be when it arrives, the

better. He should try to catch the ball just above eye level; relaxed hands and arms will 'give' gently on impact.

3. **It is easier to run in than to run back,** so he should err on the side of being too deep. On large grounds he should not always think of his position as being 'on the boundary'. His distance from the batsman will depend primarily on the estimated 'carry' of a full hit.
4. For length of return the over-arm throw is best. The higher the throw, the longer the time taken. Throws should always be as flat as possible: even reaching the wicket-keeper first bounce.

MID-OFF

There will normally be a mid-off though his position on the field may vary between wide limits. We are not concerned here with silly-mid-off, except to suggest that this position can easily be overplayed and leads to a side virtually fielding with ten men. All too often a silly-mid-off is persisted with on a good wicket, when there is no apparent prospect of a catch and when the initiative has clearly passed to the batsman. For the normal mid-off the main qualifications are:

1. Ability to start and move quickly to cut off the drive and to anticipate a quick single from 'the push'.
2. Courage to get the body and hands behind anything hit hard to him, either on the ground or in the air.
3. An accurate, flat return over medium distances.

His position will be determined by the pace of the ground, the bowler, the batsman and the position of the other off-side fielders, e.g. if there is a short extra-cover, mid-off will be deeper and straighter. The faster the ground, the deeper he can stand to a batsman who is ready to drive, and still be able to save a single.

When fielding to an away-swing, left-arm orthodox spin, or leg-break bowler, he will tend to stand wider than normal. He should remember also that drives from bowlers of this kind will tend to veer to his left.

Mid-off should back up the bowler's wicket for returns from the on-side. If the bowler is a pace bowler mid-off might have to get up to the wicket to receive returns from the on-side. This is especially true when a batsman first comes in and is often nervous until he is 'off the mark'.

There is no better place for the captain to field; he has a good view of the batsman and can discuss tactics with the bowler without interrupting the game.

MID-ON

Most of what has been written about mid-off is equally true of mid-on and indeed of mid-wicket.

When a stock bowler is attacking the off stump there will probably be no mid-wicket and mid-on will be about level with the bowler's wicket. On the other hand, when the line of attack is at the middle and leg stumps both will be required and their role will become of the utmost importance. Their positions will vary within wide limits, both in depth and in angle to the batsman, depending largely on the disposition of the other leg-side fieldsmen, the state of the pitch and the tactics of the batsmen.

Both must be ready to back-up throws from the off-side and, when there is a fast bowler, mid-on must be prepared to save the bowler's hands by getting up to the wicket to take fast returns.

THE COVERS

Traditionally the best ground fielder in the team fields at cover-point. On a fast wicket and to bowling directed at, or outside, the off stump, the covers are the most spectacular places in the field and offer the greatest scope for run-saving. There is often, too, the chance of a catch from a mis-hit or a slash and frequently an opportunity for a run-out.

Speed, fast reactions, and an accurate and flat throw, allied to good anticipation, are the chief qualifications for cover fielding.

The positions of cover and extra-cover must be elastic, depending upon the pace of the ground, the type of bowler and the batsman's normal stroke play. As a general principle they will start as deep as possible, consistent with saving a single. A really good cover-field can stand as much as ten paces deeper than the ordinary performer and still save a single, thus increasing the arc within which he can cut off the four, and, incidentally, tempting the batsman to risk a dangerous single. On fast grounds he can afford to stand several paces deeper than on slow, and on these the ball tends to come squarer from the bat, especially from leg-spin and out-swing bowling. On slow grounds and for off-spinners he will stand straighter.

More than any other fielders the covers will be on the move inward as the ball is bowled, with the hands very much at the ready. Directly the line of the ball from the stroke is clear this movement will be accelerated, to intercept it at the earliest possible moment. Speed and accuracy of return are essential, both for run-outs and as a general deterrent to close-run singles. Often, under stress, inexperienced covers take their eyes off the ball before they have grasped it, in an endeavour to see if there is a chance of a run-out: this should be avoided at all costs.

Though the overhand throw is easier to direct accurately, most great covers use the flat return from just below the level of the shoulder and sometimes the fast underhand method.

Returns generally should be full-pitch to the wicket-keeper, above the top of the stumps. The direct throw at the stumps at the bowler's end is justified if there is a fair chance of a run-out.

Experienced covers will not throw flat out unless there is a possibility of a run-out, but can gain valuable practice by throwing to the wicket-keeper on most occasions after they have fielded the ball.

THIRD-MAN

On fast grounds and to certain bowlers this is an important position. If the batsmen are running well between the wickets only a good fielder can cut off frequent singles or, if he is fielding deep to a fast bowler, prevent twos. Speed of foot and accuracy and pace of return are therefore the chief qualifications for this position.

The faster the ground and the bowling, the finer and deeper will third-man stand. But his angle to the wicket will also depend on the batsman's stroke play: early in the innings he will tend to stand finer: as the innings progresses, squarer. If he is forced to drop back, the deeper he goes the wider the arc he can cover, but he should always attempt to save two, to any ball which he can intercept.

The technique for fielding short third-man is roughly the same as for the covers, and when he is back it is the same as for the out-fields. He should remember that a ball edged to third-man always carries spin and tends to veer to his left.

Backing-up by third-man can be important if there are wild returns from the on-side.

FIELDSMEN CLOSE TO THE WICKET

THE SHORT-LEGS

This section may well begin with a word of warning. Close leg-side fielders are at times seen in first-class cricket and it is often assumed that this is normal field placing. **This is an error, for it can only be justified for a bowler who, whether by swing or spin, is bringing the ball in to the batsman: moreover it must assume a high degree of accuracy in both length and direction on the part of the bowler:** without it the field will be unbalanced and the close fielders will be liable to injury. The qualifications necessary for close fielders have already been mentioned in the section on catching – quick reactions and an ability to concentrate for long periods of time. In addition a short-leg fielder needs genuine courage to stand close knowing there is a chance of a full-blooded hit coming in his direction.

It is difficult to lay down a rule as to the normal position of short-legs either in depth or in angle to the batsman. This will depend upon the pace of the pitch, the newness of the ball, the type of bowling and whether there are other close leg-side fielders. **In depth it can be said at once that no one**

should ever be so close to the wicket that he cannot sight the ball from a firm hit: this applies particularly to a boy because of the risk of real physical injury. When behind the wicket the fieldsman should stand rather deeper, and the finer he is the deeper he should be, since the ball tends to carry further from the edge of the bat.

Short-leg fielders well behind the wicket may attempt to sight the ball momentarily from the bowler's hand and then focus on the batsman: in this way it may be possible to anticipate the likely line of the ball from the bat; those square or in front of the wicket should only focus on the batsman.

Short-leg fieldsmen must be ready to chase any ball that is pushed past them: by being able to chase and return as nearly as possible in one movement, they may often have the chance of a run-out, for batsmen are apt to misjudge short runs on the leg-side. They must also be prepared to back up the nearest wicket for throws from the off-side.

THE SLIPS

As with all close fieldsmen, a slip must command great powers of concentration.

The number and positioning of the slips will vary according to the pace of the wicket, the type of bowler and the extent to which any of them, either by spin or swing, is moving the ball away from the bat. For example, on an easy-pace wicket a medium-pace bowler who is not moving the ball will not be justified in having more than one slip, whereas on a turning wicket a slow bowler who is spinning the ball away from the batsman will probably need two.

The depth of the slips will depend not only on the bowler and the pitch, but also on the bounce: the greater the bounce, the deeper they must stand: **the criterion must be the probable 'carry' of a snick off a good length ball.**

First-slip will be the deepest; the others will be rather closer to the bat, since the thicker the edge, the less likely the ball to carry.

As regards their distance from each other: if they are too near they will be in danger of overlapping and interfering with each other's catches: there should be a small gap between their outstretched hands.

First-slip must beware of standing too fine, especially when the wicket-keeper is standing back, because the latter should move across to take any ball within reach.

It is generally agreed that first-slip should watch the ball all the way from the bowler's hand: whether second-slip should do so will depend upon how fine he is standing: if he is wide he should watch the flight of the ball initially and then focus on the outside edge of the bat.

Though it is generally true in all catching that two hands are safer than one, there are times, especially for the slips, when only a one-handed dive sideways or forwards can hope to get to the ball in time to make a catch.

Whilst a slip must always be expecting the ball to come to him he must never move to anticipate its line or height.

GULLY

Perhaps more than any other close catcher, gully depends upon fast reactions. Most of his catches will come from slashes off the meat of the bat, or from thick edges which are almost impossible to anticipate. Fast reactions and courage must therefore be high amongst his qualifications. As with the slips, the position of gully depends upon the bowler, the pitch and the batsman. For example, when fielding to a bowler spinning the ball away from the batsman on a turning pitch, he will stand quite close and square, expecting to deal mainly with edged strokes from balls which have spun and possibly lifted: on an easy-paced wicket he will stand finer and deeper to the medium-pace bowler, expecting sliced catches from mis-timed cuts and drives.

So that the gully can anticipate the likely type of catch he should learn, initially, to focus on the batsman's feet and bat. Early observation of the ball will give him some idea of the length and by watching the batsman he will be able to decide whether he is likely to get a catch from a slash or from a defensive stroke. Both slips and gully must be ready to back-up the keeper for throws from the on-side.

FIELDING PRACTICE

Quite apart from anything a coach may achieve by instruction and organized practice, players can do a great deal for themselves, if only they are keen enough, or made keen enough, to keep on playing with the ball and so acquiring 'ball sense'. Even a small boy on his own can learn to stop and catch a ball by throwing it against a wall, and to throw it accurately by aiming at a target chalked on the wall. Similarly, the coach should encourage all his players to practise amongst themselves in any spare moments, suggesting that they follow the lines of organized practice and competition by which he is trying to train them.

Confidence is a great asset in fielding and much harm can be done if, in the early stages of the season, hands are bruised. For that reason, before hands are hardened, or on cold days, the coach should use old or 'podgy' balls for fielding practice. It is important to make a friend of the ball rather than an enemy. Even tennis balls can be used for quite young players, for the technique of judging and positioning can be learnt as well with them as with a match ball. Experienced players, too, can benefit from catching practice with a tennis ball, for the hands have to be used with sensitivity and skill to prevent the ball from bouncing out. As an initial warming-up practice the coach or captain can divide his group into pairs or threes and for a few moments make them throw quick underhand catches to each other over a distance of eight to ten paces, whilst he checks for such faults as unnecessary head movement, bad balance, or wrong positioning of the hands. This practice can be turned into a small competition – 'How many catches can you make in thirty seconds?' 'Can you beat your previous score?' etc. Then he will get down to business.

For a 'full dress' fielding practice, six or seven are the ideal number: it is uneconomical in time to have larger groups. In each group there will be a batsman, a wicket-keeper properly padded and gloved behind a stump, and a fieldsman to back-up the keeper: the remainder will be dispersed in a semi-circle with their backs to the sun, if any, and the best available stretch of turf in front of them.

If necessary the coach should himself demonstrate the correct technique in catching, stopping and returning the ball, emphasizing the coaching points. He will correct faults in each of these skills before going on to the next. When hitting each ball the batsman must call out the name of the fielder for whom it is intended. Each ball, whether fielded or caught, should be returned whenever possible full pitch to the wicket-keeper. It is important to emphasize that this final act of fielding is just as vital as the stop or pick-up. Younger players might be encouraged to throw first bounce to the keeper.

At the start each hit should be well within the compass of the fieldsmen, but gradually their pace, height, or direction should be increased, e.g. low fast catches hit with slice will be sent to potential cover fielders, whilst towards the end of each session catches will be hit to the deep fielders. Occasionally this will be done both 'down and up wind' and even 'down sun'. It should be stressed that the ball should be sighted and the flight judged before moving. To practise quick sighting and judging of catches, the coach may make his fielders stand with their backs to him and not look round until they hear the ball hit and their name called. The close fielders, particularly short-legs, should be given special ground fielding practice, the ball being hit from short range, ten to twelve paces.

The close fieldsmen can practise at the slip cradle if one is available; this is best used if a blanket is stretched across the middle of it, suspended from a height of about 1·5 metres (5 ft), preventing anticipation of the catch. With beginners it is more effective if they take it in turn to stand near the cradle and throw all the catches to the fielders on the opposite side. Other slip-catching aids, such as rebound nets, provide good practice.

The best slip-catching practice is provided by a fielder throwing the ball fast from a range of ten to fifteen paces and at shoulder height to the coach so that he can slice it off the bat to the waiting fielders. This practice needs accurate throwing and considerable skill on the part of the coach, but it is far nearer the real thing than practising off a cradle: it can also be used to develop exciting competition amongst the fielders. Close catching practice can be given in another way, by a thrower standing behind a fielder, who is facing a wall, the latter having to sight and catch a solid rubber or tennis ball as it rebounds from the wall. This, too, can have great value in quickening fielders' reactions and can be made competitive.

The most valuable fielding will be carried out in the middle. At first the coach will bat with someone bowling to order and he will play strokes, as he would in a match, to a team stationed in their normal positions. He may well dispense with slips and fine-leg. During the practice he should emphasize the following coaching points:

1. As the ball is bowled all except the close fielders should be moving towards the batsman: this movement will be accelerated to meet a slow moving ball, but checked if the hit is hard.
2. Fielders should be watching the ball and the bat to anticipate the line of the stroke.
3. The ball should be watched into the hands.
4. Where possible, returns should be full-pitch to the keeper: the aim should be at the wicket-keeper's head to allow for the ball to drop a little on its way to the top of the stumps.
5. Every return must be backed-up, the backer-up being at least fifteen paces away from the wicket.
6. When chasing the ball fieldsmen must run at top speed, getting alongside the ball before they stoop to pick it up.
7. Fielders must remain in their position as indicated by the captain, and not wander about.
8. Every fielder must keep an eye on both captain and bowler, to catch an unobtrusive signal for an adjustment in his position.
9. The ball should be returned to the bowler by a gentle catch at a comfortable height.

During the practice the coach will bat as in a match, although sometimes deliberately giving chances and calling for a very short run. The fielders will be encouraged to 'let fly' whenever there is a chance of a run-out. For this reason it may be as well to have a second wicket-keeper at the bowler's end, to save the latter's hands.

This match fielding practice can, at times, be combined with training batsmen in running between the wickets. This practice is sometimes called an 'open net', two batsmen playing together for ten or fifteen minutes, as in a net, but scoring runs, calling and running.

During all fielding practices the coach must encourage and comment; he must criticize when things are done wrongly but, when a good catch is made, there is a fine stop, or a fast and accurate return, he should make everyone feel he is as delighted as the fieldsman himself.

3

Wicket-Keeping

Of all positions in the field that of wicket-keeper is at once the most important and the most exacting. Not only does he have more chances than any other fielder to intervene decisively in the game by catch, stumping or run-out, but he must be keyed up to anticipate such a chance with every ball of every innings. Moreover, his form behind the stumps must have a profound effect on the morale not only of his bowlers but of the whole team: the feeling that they can rely on the skilful co-operation of their wicket-keeper will strongly reinforce the former's confidence, whilst his keenness, vitality and general competence, especially in the taking of returns, can inspire and sustain his fellows through a long outing in the field.

It can therefore be laid down as an absolute principle in team selection that the best wicket-keeper should always be chosen. The qualifications for the position are in the main the same as those necessary for any close-in fielder – quickness of eye and reaction, natural co-ordination – but to these must be added as especially desirable in his case, strong hands, physical courage and what can perhaps be described as mental, moral and physical stamina.

It is a common assumption that good wicket-keepers are born and not made, but it is far from certain that all the best potential keepers naturally take to the gloves at an early age, and a coach would be wise to let any boy who has leanings in that direction try his hand. No long trial will be needed to determine whether he is or is not likely to become a wicket-keeper, but to become one in fact demands determination, training and prolonged practice.

Equipment

Selection and care of gloves are of vital importance to the wicket-keeper's art.

New gloves tend to be stiff and unwieldy and should be worked on, to obtain flexibility and a cup effect in the palms, before using them in a match. This can be accomplished by hammering the palms with the end of an old bat and considerable ball catching in each glove. Should the rubber surface of the gloves become worn or shiny, the light use of some form of sandpaper will generally suffice until they can be re-covered. On no account should any form of dressing be used on the palms which will make the ball 'tacky' to the detriment of the bowlers, although a leather dressing may be used on the backs to help flexibility.

Inner gloves, preferably of chamois leather, should always be worn, although cotton inners can be equally effective and comfortable. Padding in the form of felt or foam rubber strips can be stuck to the face of the inners for added protection, although it is not good practice unless one is protecting slight bruising of the palm. Many wicket-keepers bind the first joints of their fingers with surgical tape to reduce the possibility of injury to these vulnerable parts of the hand. Some bind the inners themselves to give them a more compact feeling within the stalls of the main glove. If the inners are not elasticated at the wrists, elastic bands can be worn providing they are not too tight. This greatly assists the removal of the main glove when it is required to make a fast throw, in an attempt at a run-out.

Pads are merely an incidental second line of defence for a wicket-keeper and should never come into play unless by some mischance his first line has been breached. This is equally true of taking returns as of taking the bowling: activity and accuracy in taking every throw, however wild, with the hands will in itself help to tidy up the fielding. The special heavy wicket-keeping pads sometimes seen are an unnecessary encumbrance: ordinary pads are perfectly adequate. When buckling on his pads before going out in the field, the wicket-keeper should **never** tuck his trousers in his socks. Folding the trouser neatly at the top of the boot or shoe before tightening the strap presents a much neater appearance.

Comfort and lightness are the essentials of the wicket-keeper's footwear. Boots should be well studded but the studs themselves should not be too long. The reasons for this are that long studs tend to press uncomfortably on the soles of the feet, particularly when the wicket-keeper is in the squatting position. Long studs too become embedded in the turf and can cause injury to the ankle or knee when the wicket-keeper turns quickly. Providing they give an adequate grip, in dry conditions rubber-soled boots or shoes can be worn. In fact on non-turf wickets they are essential and all wicket-keepers should possess a pair. Clean woollen, well fitting socks add to the wicket-keeper's comfort during a long session in the field.

Cricket cap, athletic support and protector are other essentials of the wicket-keeper's equipment.

The cricket cap shields the eyes from the sun, particularly when taking high returns, it helps concentrate the vision, and when standing up to the wicket can be a protection against the lifting ball or swinging bat. Caps should fit well: there is nothing more untidy than seeing a cricketer in the field continually picking up his cap following the slightest movement or gust of wind. The athletic support combined with the slip-in protector is again vital for comfort and confidence, and **at no time should a wicket-keeper practise or play in a match without a protector.**

As the focal point of the team in the field the wicket-keeper should always 'look the part'. **There is no excuse for dirty or uncared-for clothing or equipment.**

THE BASIC TECHNIQUE

Position

A wicket-keeper must stand either right up or right back: there can be no half-way house. He should never hesitate to stand back to any bowling above medium pace or even to medium-paced bowling on very fast or 'lifting' pitches, if by so doing he will be improving his chance of taking the straightforward catch: for this is his first responsibility. No false pride, still less any instinct for showmanship, must weigh with him for a moment. He can be encouraged too by remembering that most fast bowlers prefer to see their wicket-keeper standing back, and that by doing so he is much less likely to unsight first-slip and very much more likely to catch the leg snick.

How far back he will stand will obviously depend on the pace of the bowler and the nature of the pitch: the faster the bowler and the livelier the pitch, the further back he will go. **But in general he will aim at so positioning himself that he can take a good length ball between knee and waist height just after it has started to drop in its trajectory after pitching.**

Should he decide to stand up he should stand so close to the wicket that, after taking the ball, in normal circumstances, he can break it without overstretching or loss of balance.

Stance

The wicket-keeper's stance should ensure:

1. **That he is comfortable and as little as possible conscious of any strain.**
2. **That he can get the best possible sight of the ball.**
3. **That he can take the ball with the minimum of movement.**

Most wicket-keepers today adopt the 'squatting' position (Fig. 1) with the seat very close to the ground and the weight evenly distributed on the balls of both feet. The eyes should be level and the back of the fingers resting lightly on the ground between the legs, fingers pointing downwards. The advantage of this position is that it minimizes muscular strain, provides the best possible sight of the ball and establishes a 'springboard' from which the wicket-keeper can move extremely quickly.

When standing up the left foot will generally be positioned behind the off and middle stumps, the right foot parallel with it a comfortable

Fig. 1.
The squatting position: balance on soles of feet: body right down, eyes level: gloves together and resting lightly on ground with fingers pointing downwards

distance away. Obviously, should the wicket-keeper not be able to sight the delivery and line of the ball from this position, due to the type of bowler or some idiosyncrasy of the batsman, he will move appropriately wider.

Whereas when standing up the wicket-keeper should stay down in the squatting position as long as possible and come up with the ball, when standing back he will have risen to the crouching position as soon as he has sighted the line and will be ready to take off in any direction. Some wicket-keepers in fact adopt the crouching rather than the squatting position as their stance when standing back.

It is most important that the head be kept still and down as long as possible, only moving with the rise of the ball off the pitch (*see* upper plate 22a). The greatest wicket-keepers have always contrived to make their art look simple: with most of them indeed it has been so unobtrusive that spectators take it for granted. This economy of movement is important for two reasons: it facilitates a true sighting of the ball and it minimizes fatigue over a long innings.

The feet

The feet should move as little as possible but always enough to ensure that the body is, as far as possible, in a balanced position behind the line of the ball.

Bertie Oldfield. A fine example of staying down: this applies particularly to a well pitched-up ball. The batsman, Walter Hammond, has driven the ball through the covers *Sydney Morning Herald*

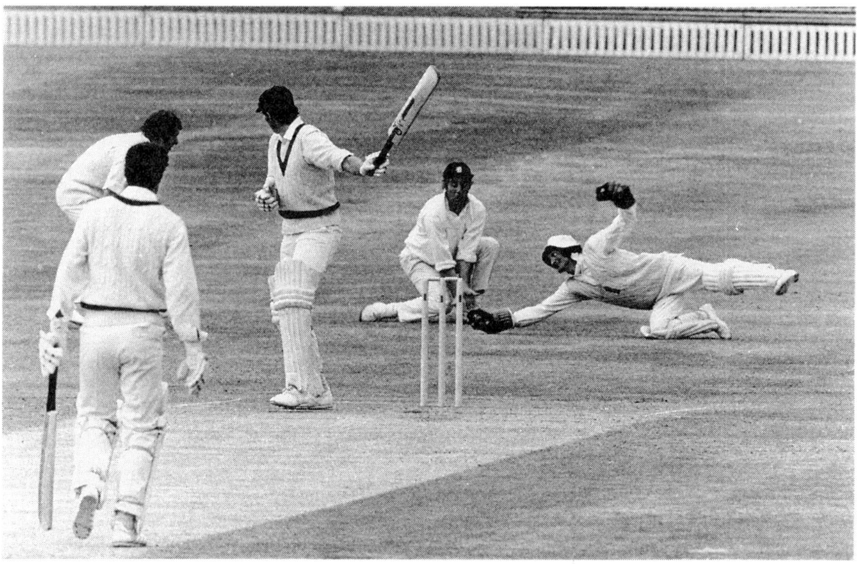

Alan Knott. Well known for his attitude towards fitness: he practises what he preaches in making this fine, low catch *Patrick Eagar*

Rod Marsh. Australia's record breaking wicket-keeper is beautifully balanced to make this stumping attempt *All-Sport/Adrian Murrell*

Bob Taylor. Another great wicket-keeper: he attacks the wicket in an effort to make a leg-side stumping, especially difficult when 'keeping' to a left-handed batsman *Patrick Eagar*

When standing up he should always endeavour to take the ball as close to the bat as possible: this particularly applies when the batsman is cutting. In taking balls to off or leg, care must be taken to ensure that **the outside foot moves over at least parallel with and never backwards away**

Fig. 2.
Taking the ball at normal height just outside the off stump: the right foot has moved across to bring the head on to the line: note the position of the hands

from the crease. It is good practice to cultivate a slight forward and inward turn of the outside foot when moving towards the line of the ball (Fig. 2). This assists the balance and poise of the body to be more easily transferred towards the stumps. In taking the ball on the leg-side it is bad practice to move the feet too early – before picking up the approximate line and length of the ball.

The body

So far as possible the body should be on, or be brought onto, the line of the ball in a balanced position.

There are a number of reasons for this: it will mean that the eyes are level and truly sighting the ball and if the hands fail to take it, it will be intercepted by the body.

Good balance is probably the most important factor in successful wicket-keeping (*see* lower plate 22a). It enables the weight to be transferred quickly towards the wicket as the ball is taken: it enables the wicket-keeper to take the lifting ball cleanly by 'moving' the head and upper body inside the line of the ball: it also enables the wicket-keeper to reach for and catch wider balls to off and leg with confidence and without fear of injury.

The hands

There are two vital principles to which the hands must conform:

1. **The fingers should never point directly at the ball** (*see* Fig. 2). Palms should face the ball allowing the fingers to point mainly downwards, but to the side or upwards if it is necessary to catch a high ball 'baseball' fashion. The hands must not be rigid but held in a relaxed cup with the feeling that they are padded cushions into which the ball will sink.
2. **The hands should 'ride' with the ball,** that is to say, carry back several inches as it enters them: thus minimizing the tendency for the ball to jump out as well as the risk of bruising. Care should be taken, however, not to exaggerate this movement.

On cold days hands should be warmed before taking the field: this can be accomplished by soaking them in warm water. At the end of a long session in the field slight bruising of the palms will be eased by similar treatment.

Concentration

So far we have been concerned with the pure mechanics of wicket-keeping, but they will be of no avail unless they are reinforced by **the most relentless concentration and the most vigilant watching of the ball.** This must become an instinctive habit, but will only do so if he constantly strives for it.

The wicket-keeper must assume that every ball will reach him, even the most comfortable full-pitch which it would seem impossible for the batsman to miss.

Like the batsman, he must watch the bowler's hand and watch the ball not only in the air but off the pitch. To do this effectively and to go on doing it, he must banish everything else from his mind. He must never be upset by set-backs, nor must he be deluded by success into thinking his job easy: it never is. Of course, he will miss more catches than other fielders, for he will get more: what matters is the proportion of reasonable chances that he accepts.

Stumping

In the majority of cases when a stumping is missed the failure is due to one or other of three very natural temptations:

1. Looking at the bat and assuming the ball will hit it.
2. Looking up before the ball is taken, i.e. taking one's eye off the ball.
3. Snatching at the ball.

The wicket-keeper should avoid stumping preoccupation, which will lead him to watch the batsman rather than the ball. **If he takes the ball correctly the breaking of the wicket will follow naturally.**

Experience will create an instinct for the type of stroke that may provide a stumping chance: sometimes the wicket-keeper will break the wicket only to find the batsman has never left, or is back in, his ground. This should not deter him from repeating his effort should he feel the opportunity is there. **He should always be looking for the chance of a dismissal,** but at the same time should not break the wicket or appeal unnecessarily.

Taking returns from the field

Accuracy and agility by the wicket-keeper in taking returns from the field are not only essential for affecting run-outs but are of high importance in sustaining general morale and in deterring batsmen from taking short runs. He must always position himself close to the stumps, facing directly down the line of the returns. To do this, if he is standing back, will mean a very quick start from his original position. The technique for taking the ball will be the same as if it came from the bowler.

However inaccurate the throw-in the wicket-keeper must try to take it cleanly in his gloves and never be content to stop it with his pads.

The wicket-keeper is in an excellent position to make run-outs when the ball is played for sharp singles near the striker's wicket. He should never be afraid of chasing the ball quickly, removing the glove from his throwing hand and aiming at the wicket where the run-out is most likely to be achieved.

When the ball goes into the outfield it can be useful, particularly when there are a number of close-in fielders, for the wicket-keeper to raise an arm as a guide for the thrower.

Practice

Whilst there is no substitute for match experience in taking all types of bowling on all types of wicket, a good deal can be done for the young wicket-keeper in other ways. Correct taking of the ball can be simply practised by asking someone to throw the ball to him, varying its length and direction, at a range of between ten to twenty paces. He can practise by himself with a tennis or similar ball, throwing it at a rough wall from which the rebound will vary in pace and direction.

Catching games with other players are always fun. Particularly good practice can be obtained using a rebound net or a slip cradle over which an available piece of material such as canvas is stretched to prevent the catcher seeing and thus anticipating the direction and speed of the catch. There is no reason why wicket-keepers should not take advantage of the team net practice, as described in the chapter on 'Net Practice'. Treated properly net practice can be an excellent way of getting to know your team bowlers.

Fitness

There was a time when at the Team Trial the wicket-keeper was 'selected' after the more mobile players had been elected to their position. Fortunately, this is no longer the case as **the one attribute expected of the wicket-keeper is fitness and mobility.** There are many games and exercises that can help in reaching and maintaining a good standard of fitness, some of which are described in the chapter 'Fitness for Cricket'. It is perhaps worth mentioning the game of squash as being particularly suitable for the wicket-keeper.

Whilst shunning any form of showmanship a wicket-keeper must by his activity and general tidiness make himself felt behind the wicket as a focus to the fielding side. He should expect and encourage his fielders to throw in fast and accurately to him, even when no run is attempted. It will keep him warm and agile, it will give them the range and it will make the batsman think.

If a catch is skied near the wicket and the captain does not, as he should, call him by name, the wicket-keeper must not hesitate to shout 'Mine' loudly and clearly and go for the catch: once he does so he should go on with his attempt at all costs.

He must learn to throw the ball accurately to the bowler or to the nearest fielder. It is criminal to make the bowler stoop!

If at any time his hands become really bruised, he should take a rest from wicket-keeping at once, rather than try to hang on and risk being out of the game for much longer. He should always ensure that sleeves cover the elbows: they can save a nasty skinning when diving for the ball.

Outside the basic techniques of wicket-keeping previously described, successful wicket-keepers over the years have developed variations and refinements to their art that should not be ignored. What suits one may not suit another, but practice and enthusiasm will prompt young wicket-keepers to study others and develop their own style.

It is said that the most satisfying dismissal is the leg-side stumping. This may be true for the connoisseur but the spectacular one-handed diving catch must be a close second. Wicket-keepers should be encouraged to go wholeheartedly after any ball they think they can catch and whilst two hands are better than one, the really wide deflection must be tried for with one hand. The extra distance that can be covered is considerable (*see* upper plate 22b). When standing back it is wise for the wicket-keeper to ask first-slip to stand wide enough to allow him to go for the ball without hesitation. This gives the wicket-keeper confidence and, further, allows the slips to cover a greater catching area.

The wicket-keeper in his exacting and sometimes thankless role has probably the greatest opportunity for really full enjoyment of the game. He is totally involved and if blessed with a good sense of humour and the spirit never to stop trying – what an asset he will be to his team – win or lose.

Common faults

1. **Standing in 'no man's land', neither right up nor right back.**
2. **Snatching or grabbing at the ball.**
3. **Taking one's eye off the ball.**
4. **Getting up too early when standing up to the wicket.**
5. **Moving to either side too early – before picking up the true line of the ball.**
6. **Excessive head movement.**
7. **Taking the ball off balance.**
8. **Incorrect weight distribution when attempting to break the wicket.**
9. **Casual or even lazy footwork.**
10. **Fingers rather than palms pointing at the ball.**
11. **Hesitation in going for wide balls.**
12. **Unnecessary use of pads.**
13. **Bad returns to bowler or fielder.**
14. **Badly cared-for equipment.**
15. **Loss of concentration.**

4

Bowling

No matter how many runs a cricket team makes it cannot win a match until its opponents have been dismissed. The better the class of cricket, and the better the pitch, the more true it is that whilst the batsman saves matches, it is the bowler, assisted by his fielders, who wins them. In Test Match cricket the series has been determined far more often by superiority in bowling than in batting.

Bowling is not a natural technique any more than is batting. It has to be learnt and practised; but whereas both demand a certain degree of physical co-ordination, the bowler need not be born with the quickness of eye and reaction that are necessary to become an outstanding batsman. **Given a reasonable start by sound teaching, the opportunity to practise, some intelligence, but above all real determination and enthusiasm, most boys can become good enough to enjoy bowling and to be of value as bowlers to their side.**

Each will eventually make up his own mind how he wants to bowl, but a coach can help to guide his choice wisely. In the sections that follow some suggestions are made as to the physical and mental qualifications that make for success in different types of bowling. But whichever type a boy decides to adopt, a coach must try to impress on him that bowling is not just mechanical, but a craft and an art, demanding real study and application; above all, that it can only be mastered by practice. There is no easy way.

The aim of the bowler, whether he is fast, medium or slow, is to defeat the batsman opposed to him: it may be by the direct assault of pace, by the deception of spin and flight, by sheer persistency, or by a combination of all these. But to do this economically **he must be able to command accuracy in length and direction.**

Only by experience will he learn what is good length. In broad terms a good length ball is one which brings into the mind of the batsman a degree of uncertainty whether to play forward or back and in either case it can only be played defensively if played straight. Good length will, of course, be relative to the pace of the pitch, the pace and height of the bowler and the reach of the batsman.

As he starts his run-up for each ball the bowler should have a clear mental picture of what he wants and means to bowl: the more he can convince himself that he can, and is going to bowl the ball he wants, the more likely he is to bowl it: this confidence is a great asset in bowling and can be built up during practice.

The bowler must constantly remind himself that the initiative lies with him. and that he must do everything he can to retain it. Whatever his method of attack, it must be inspired and sustained by a proper hostility to the batsman.

By encouragement and suggestion the coach can do much to reinforce a bowler's resolution and to increase his resource, but the greatest service he can do him will be to help him to bowl with a good action.

THE BASIC ACTION

Bowling actions vary in practice as greatly as batting styles, but there are certain fundamentals which are essential to success. Though some good bowlers, and even a few great bowlers, may seem to violate some of these fundamentals, they are good in spite of, not because of, such violations, which are generally more apparent than real.

As will be indicated in the separate sections, each type of bowler may need to make minor adjustments to the basic action in order to deliver a particular type of ball.

The fundamentals of a good bowling action are:

1. **A correct grip.**
2. **A smooth and economical run-up.**
3. **An easy, rhythmical and well balanced delivery, making full use of height and body.**
4. **A deliberate and fluent follow-through.**

It must be emphasized that the following detailed information is needed much more by the coach than by the bowler. The coach must have this information if he is to assess the action of a bowler and diagnose the cause of any faults in it, whereas if a bowler becomes too aware of the individual phases of his action he may lose spontaneity and, therefore, his rhythm. The correct action can be achieved if the bowler is made aware of the simple basic coaching points, but neither the bowler nor the coach should consider more than one or two of these points at a time.

N.B. Everything that follows is written for a right-arm bowler: for a left-armer reverse 'left' and 'right'.

The grip

The grip of the ball will, of course, vary according to the type of ball which the bowler intends to deliver: such variations in grip will be discussed later. **But for all types of bowling it is essential that the ball should be held in the**

fingers and not in the palm of the hand. Only so can the bowler have full control of the ball. It is the fingers which, as the final extension of the wrist and hand, impart that whip which, in turn, gives the ball 'life' off the pitch.

Fig. 1. A basic grip

The run-up

As already stated, the bowler should have a clear idea before he starts his run-up, what he intends to bowl. During the run-up he should watch the batsmen and then concentrate on the line and length of the intended delivery or alternatively on the spot where he intends to pitch the ball. This may also help him to keep his head still.

The object of the run-up is to bring the bowler to the bowling crease completely balanced and with the momentum necessary to bowl, and keep on bowling, at his normal designed pace. Its length should be the minimum necessary to provide this momentum. It should be smooth, rhythmical and regular without hops or changes of step.

The run should 'build up' – in other words the bowler should start slowly, even walking the first pace or two, and then gradually increase his speed: **it is only in the last few strides that the full momentum should be reached.**

The balance of the body should be slightly forward and carried on the front of the feet. The muscles should be relaxed but there should be throughout a feeling of 'tidiness' and control.

During the last stride of the run-up prior to the delivery stride, the body is gathered for a jump off the left foot. This jump (sometimes called 'the bound') gives height and, therefore, the time in the air needed for the body to turn from a position facing down the wicket to one which is sideways to it. The shoulders start the turn and are automatically followed by the hips and legs. The head, however, remains still and facing down the pitch.

As the bowler jumps he must feel that the right leg is leading the body

Dennis Lillee. 'The spring is cocked': weight well back and body sideways; head perfectly poised *Patrick Eagar*

Kapil Dev. The perfect landing: right foot parallel to the crease, body sideways, back slightly arched, left arm high *All-Sport/Adrian Murrell*

Dennis Lillee. The beginning of the delivery stride: left shoulder and arm pointing down the pitch, head still looking over left shoulder *Patrick Eagar*

Neil Foster. The beginning of the follow-through: right shoulder now pointing down the pitch, eyes still looking at the batsman *All-Sport/Adrian Murrell*

into the air. It is the leading right leg which causes the bowler to lean backwards, i.e. away from the batsman as he starts his delivery.

The delivery

During his delivery a bowler passes through an infinite number of positions. Five of these have been chosen for the purpose of analysis. **Although these key positions have been selected, they are in no sense static positions, but should be thought of more as high-speed photographs.** It cannot be over-emphasized that the bowler passes through these positions and never 'holds' any of them.

In broad principle the first two positions represent the winding up of the body: the third and fourth positions its unwinding and the release of the ball: the fifth occurs during the follow-through. Any minor errors in the early positions usually lead to major faults in the later positions. Each is dependent upon its predecessor.

It is the bowler's ability to co-ordinate the correct movements of the body, arms and feet, that gives rhythm and timing to the delivery: without these the bowler will lack 'life' off the pitch and accuracy in length and direction.

The following analysis applies to a bowler of medium pace: but the general principles will be found to hold good for all types of bowling.

POSITION 1

Position 1 occurs just after the jump off the left foot and whilst the body is in the air. The shoulders are sideways, pointing down the pitch. The right leg is passing in front of the left: this is called 'crossing in front'. The right foot is turning so that it will land parallel to the bowling crease. The left arm is slightly bent and ready to swing upwards: the right hand is about level with the face.

POSITION 2 – THE 'COIL' POSITION

Position 2 occurs on landing. The body has completed a half-turn so that the left shoulder and hips are pointing down the pitch. The right foot has landed parallel to the crease: the back is slightly arched: the front arm, though not rigid, is extended upwards as high as possible and the bowler is looking down the pitch from behind it. The weight is on the back foot and the body is leaning away from the batsman with the front leg raised and bent slightly: the right arm (the bowling arm) is about to swing forward and down past the chest at the start of the delivery swing.

There is a good reason for all this. The right foot landing parallel to the crease ensures a full sideways turn of the body with the left shoulder

The Basic Action: position 1

pointing down the pitch: this will produce the maximum pivot. The arching of the back and the body inclining away from the batsman will, in effect, hold the body back so that it can exert the maximum force in the delivery phase: the high knee position can only be achieved if the body is leaning away from the batsman. The left arm is ready to lead the forward swing of the body.

Position 2 is of the utmost importance since it represents the completion of the winding-up of the body; errors at this stage can seldom, if ever, be compensated. The spring is now cocked and ready for release.

The 'delivery stride' now takes place. As the body swings forward, led by the

The Basic Action: position 2

left arm being thrown out and down towards the batsman and with the left shoulder pointing down the pitch, the fully extended right arm will start to come up: this movement of the arms will now be rather like a cartwheel.

POSITION 3

The weight is about to be transferred from the back foot to the front foot which has not quite reached the ground.

The left shoulder and arm are still pointing down the pitch, the back is arched, and the head is looking along this arm.

The left foot will land flat and in line with the back foot: it should never land to the off-side, i.e. to the left of that line: if it lands appreciably to the on-side, i.e. to the right of that line, it will interfere with the follow-through. The left foot will naturally point towards fine-leg.

The length of the 'delivery stride' must depend upon the speed of the approach to the crease and the physique of the bowler: naturally a fast bowler will have a longer stride than a slower bowler: its function is to provide a firm and adequate base for the delivery. Too short a stride may result in the bowler transferring his weight too soon: too long a stride will result in loss of height.

The Basic Action: position 3

As the left leg lands it will 'give' slightly but it must immediately begin to straighten and so assist the body into the delivery action.

The body will now begin to pivot. It will start around the left leg and then, as the full weight is taken on this leg, it will continue around the whole left side: it will be seen first at the hips and then at the shoulders. The continuing swing of the left arm down and backwards, close to the left side, together with the upwards swing of the right arm (the bowling arm) will bring the left shoulder below the right at the instant of delivery.

If the unwinding of the body starts too early, the bowler will not only fail to make use of his pivot at the vital moment, but will reach the point of

delivery too soon, and thus bowl mainly with his arm. Whilst all bowlers deliver the ball with the hips and shoulders square to the batsman, it is bowlers with these faults who are described as 'open-chested' or 'arm bowlers'. The front arm swinging down wide of the left side, or the head not being kept as still as possible, will contribute to this and may also result in the left shoulder falling away to the off-side. All or any of these faults will destroy the rhythm and timing of the action upon which power and accuracy so largely depend.

POSITION 4

This is the instant when the ball is released. The full weight of the body will now be firmly over the front leg and the body will still be pivoting around the left side. Slow bowlers will find the front leg is almost, if not completely, straight: faster bowlers will find it approaching a straight position. The

The Basic Action: position 4

hips will be square to the front and the shoulders will have caught up with the hips so that the chest is also square to the batsman. **The bowler will now be able to release the ball with the left side firm and from the greatest possible height. The head will be over or slightly in front of the left foot and the eyes will still be looking down the pitch.**

POSITION 5

This is the beginning of the follow-through and will reflect the efficiency of the run-up and delivery.

Because of the faster rotation of the upper part of the body, **the right shoulder will now be pointing down the pitch and the bowler will be looking at the batsman over this shoulder.**

The front arm will have completed a full circle and the bowling arm will have been carried past the hips close to the body.

As the weight is carried beyond the left leg, the bowler will travel on to the right leg, which will have been picked up and carried forward flexed at the knee. **This leg must not swing wide,** thus unbalancing the body and

The Basic Action: position 5

causing it to fall away to the off-side. **The head must not drop sideways and the bowler will continue to look down the pitch.**

But the action is still not completed. The follow-through must be continued, its length naturally depending on the pace of the bowler; if it is not, the action will be stunted and the rhythm lost. In these final strides **the bowler must not turn away too sharply to the off-side: at the same time he must be careful not to run on to the pitch:** this not only transgresses the Laws of the game but, once acquired, a fault is difficult to eradicate.

Common faults

1. Not having a consistent and gradually accelerating run-up which allows for a good jump off the left foot. Inconsistencies may lead to:
   (*a*) the right foot passing behind the left, i.e. 'crossing behind' (*see* Position 1)
   (*b*) hopping into the delivery stride, i.e. taking off and landing on the right foot rather than jumping from the left foot onto the right.
2. The jump not giving sufficient height and rotation: this fault is often the cause of many subsequent errors.
3. Not landing with the right foot parallel to the bowling crease, i.e. insufficient turn of the shoulders at the instant of take-off (*see* Position 2).
4. No arching of the back and an insufficient lean-back of the body, i.e. away from the batsman (*see* Position 2).
5. Bowling off the wrong foot: this is caused by a combination of 2 and 4 above. Bowlers with this fault almost always land with the right foot pointing down the pitch.
6. The left arm not climbing high enough (*see* Position 2).
7. The head not looking down the pitch from behind the front arm (*see* Position 2).
8. The front foot landing too wide and splaying to the off-side (*see* Position 3).
9. Poor use of the front arm: if the front arm swings forward and around in a horizontal plane, the bowling arm will probably not be as high as possible in the instant of release (*see* Position 4).
10. An inadequate follow-through thus losing rhythm (*see* Position 5).
11. A lack of concentration – not fixing the eyes and mind on the line and length to be bowled.

THE COACH AND THE BOWLER

Possibly the most difficult issues with regard to cricket coaching are those involving the Bowling Action. **To help the coach diagnose faults in a bowler's**

action it is necessary to analyse and evaluate each stage of it. In order to do this he should observe carefully several deliveries paying attention to only one phase. The first phase to be examined should be the run-up: is it smooth, is is too fast etc.? When the coach is satisfied that he has gleaned all he can about the run-up, he should progress to the next phase – the jump into the delivery stride. As his evaluation continues he should make mental or written notes to remind himself of what requires attention and also what can profitably be left alone.

The attention should now be focused on each of the Five Basic Positions in turn to discover if the bowler passes through them before finally scrutinizing the length and direction of the follow-through. Only at this point should the coach make his decision regarding any faults and more important the cause of the fault.

Before insisting that a bowler make major or radical changes in his action the coach should be quite certain that:

1. The bowler's present action accounts for his lack of success.
2. The changes to be made will markedly improve the bowler.
3. Sufficient time is available to enable the coach and the bowler to achieve the desired effect.
4. The bowler is aware of his faults and wishes to make the required effort to eradicate them.

If any of the above conditions cannot be met the coach would be well advised to concentrate on polishing up the present action by minor adjustments.

Even small alterations, a different grip, slightly higher arm action, etc. may well have an adverse effect for a short time and both the coach and player should be aware that a drop in the level of performance could be experienced for some time.

Coaching is an art not a science and any advice should only be given after due regard to the ability, age, experience and aptitude of the individual at whom it is directed. Far too many bowlers have suffered from inexperienced or dogmatic coaches, who could not discern that which was good but deviated from the basic principles in some way and should be left alone, from that which was patently bad and definitely in need of early correction.

SWING

Every fast, medium or even slow bowler whose action conforms to the principles just analysed can make the ball swing, provided the conditions are suitable and the ball is gripped correctly. Sometimes, indeed, they will find it difficult to prevent the ball from swinging. **But the ability to make the ball 'move in the air' is of little value unless it is combined with**

Harold Larwood. Perfectly poised for the delivery stride *The Photo Source/Central Press*

Alec Bedser. The perfect follow-through

accuracy – accuracy of length and, perhaps even more important, of direction.

Swing must not be used without thought, or the batsman may become acclimatized and adjust his strokes to it. It should be varied by a change of pace and by bowling an occasional straight one, perhaps with the fingers across rather than down the seam, and also by bowling the ball from different positions on the crease.

Given favourable conditions it is not difficult to bowl both out-swing and in-swing, but to do so successfully requires real control of direction. Young bowlers had much better concentrate on one or the other and set their field accordingly, possibly making use of a cutter for variation (*see* below).

Certain conditions favour swing bowling:

1. A heavy atmosphere.
2. A wind from the appropriate quarter.
3. A new, or relatively new, ball, with a still prominent seam: the bowler must, therefore, keep the seam as clean as possible. The fielders must co-operate in trying to keep the shine on the ball for as long as possible, by keeping the ball off the ground.

A brief explanation of the principles of swing may help the bowler to understand the importance of using his body and bowling hand in order to release the ball at the correct angle.

a. The axis of the ball must be vertical and the seam must point in the direction of the intended swing.

b. The position of the seam must be stable. The seam is stabilized by back spin: this is imparted naturally, if the ball is released correctly.

c. The ball swings more consistently if one side of the ball is more highly polished than the other (*see* upper diagrams Fig. 2 overleaf).

As the ball travels through the air, so the air 'splits' on the seam. The air on the smooth, shiny side flows past the ball relatively undisturbed. The air flow on the rougher side of the ball, and on the seam, becomes turbulent. The differing air flow exerts different pressures on each side of the ball – and thus causes the ball to swing. A ball travelling more slowly is more susceptible to the change in pressure, and thus swings more easily. A lighter ball, e.g. $4\frac{3}{4}$ ounces (134·6 grams), is also more susceptible to the change in pressure (*see* lower diagram Fig. 2 overleaf).

OUT-SWING

Although in-swing is more commonly bowled than out-swing, nearly all good batsmen are agreed that it is the ball which 'leaves them' late in its flight which is the more difficult to play, and the bowler who can command it in his opening overs may well strike a vital blow for his side.

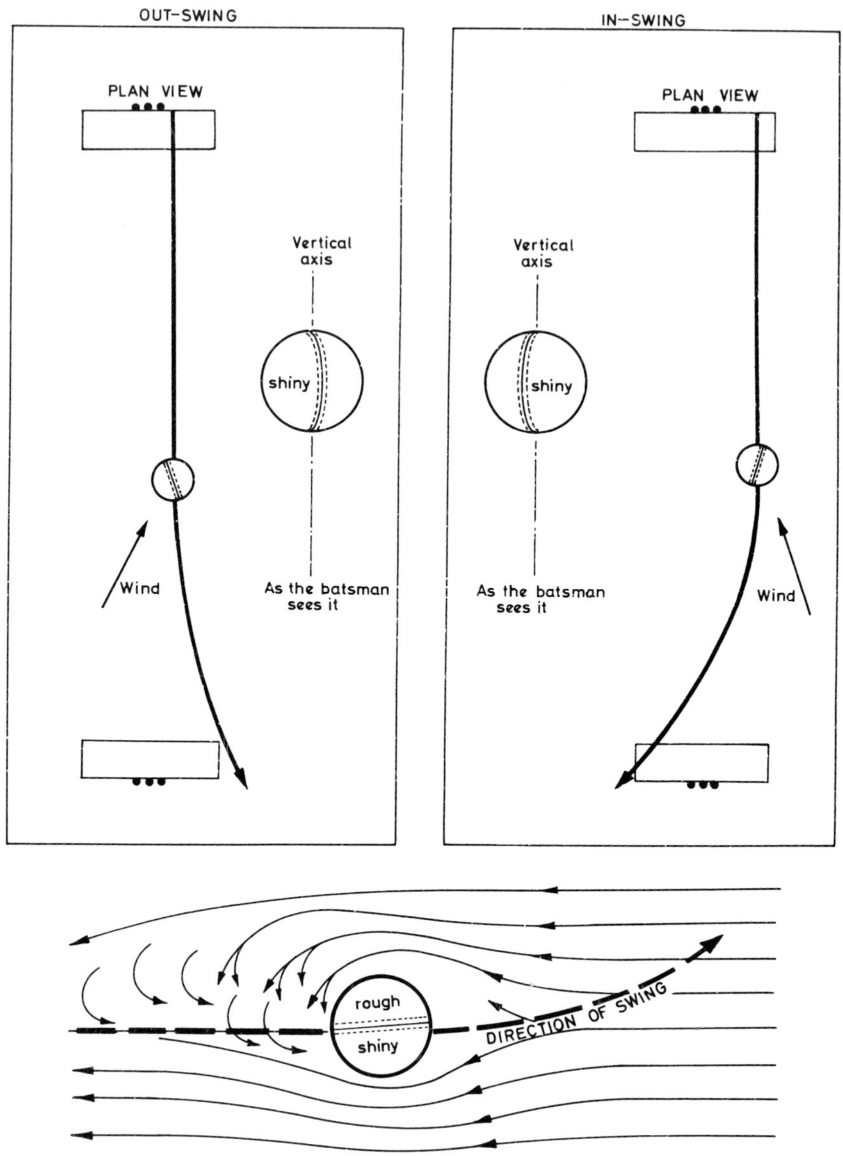

Fig. 2. The theory of swing

The grip

Every bowler must work out for himself the exact grip which suits his own action best: but in the main it will conform to the following:

1. The seam is angled slightly in the direction of the intended swing, i.e. towards first-slip.
2. The first and second fingers will be on top of the ball roughly on each side of the seam. With the ball thus angled, however, they must obviously lie slightly across it: the right side of the thumb will be directly beneath it (Fig. 3).

At the moment of release the seam must be vertical and angled in the direction of the intended swing. Whilst the angling of the seam undoubtedly helps to promote swing, it may also tend to start the swing too early in the ball's flight: in which case the seam should be made to point more directly down the pitch. In any event it is probable that all bowlers will find it necessary to experiment from time to time, even from day to day, with minor adjustments in the angle of the seam.

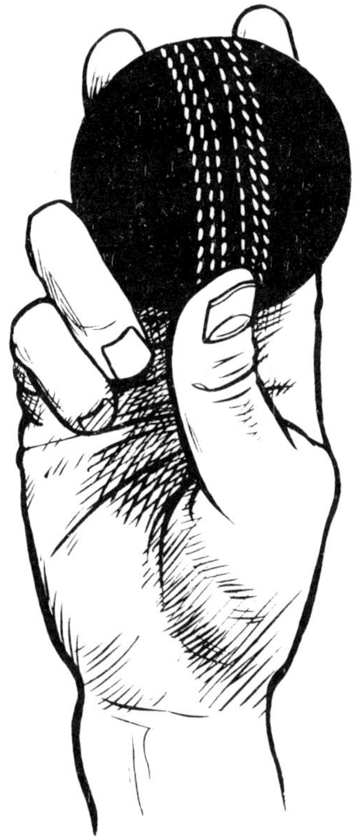

Fig. 3. Grip for out-swing

The action

For out-swing the rotation of the shoulders should be slightly exaggerated. The extra turn of the shoulders will be obtained as the bowler jumps off the left foot, and will be seen as he lands in Position 2 of the Basic Bowling Action. The back foot will be at least parallel to the bowling crease, and the front foot may land slightly across the line of direction, i.e. to the on-side of it. The batsman will therefore see rather more of the bowler's left shoulder. **There will be a greater pivot around the front leg thus resulting in a more pronounced follow-through in which the right hand must swing down and across the body to finish close to the left side of the thigh.**

The wrist should be kept a little stiffer than for a normal delivery, and the bowler should feel, as his arm comes over, that his first two fingers are kept behind the ball for as long as possible: to assist this action the wrist should be kept firm, well into the follow-through.

It is easier to bowl the out-swinger from close to the stumps, but if a bowler can also bowl it from wider on the crease and still make it swing sufficiently, it is a more difficult ball to play, because of its angle of approach to the batsman.

Use of out-swing

The bowler must bowl straight enough to make the batsman play at the ball, and, if possible, make him play forward. There are two reasons for this: if the batsman is allowed to play off the back foot, he has more time to watch the ball and judge its line: the further up the ball is pitched, the more 'time' it has in which to swing.

To waste the new ball is a bowling crime: it not only gives the batsman a free sight of the swing, but it takes the shine off the ball and tires the bowler to no effect.

IN-SWING

Many bowlers find it easier to make the ball swing in than out, perhaps because they do not have a sufficient pivot of the shoulders during the delivery stride. **However, for in-swing the bowler needs to have even greater control of length and direction than for out-swing.** The inaccurate in-swing bowler is likely to be expensive and may well be a menace to his close leg-side fielders, but bowling accurately and supported by good catching, he can be invaluable.

The grip

As with out-swing, bowlers must experiment for themselves, especially with the angle of the seam, but the normal grip will be as follows:

1. The seam is angled slightly in the direction of the intended swing, i.e. to fine-leg.
2. The first and second fingers will lie on top of the ball, one on each side of the seam: the ball of the thumb will be placed directly under the seam (Fig. 4).

The action

For in-swing the rotation of the shoulders will be rather less than for out-swing. **As the bowler lands in the 'coil' position the batsman may see less of the bowler's left side, and perhaps a little of the right shoulder: the arching of the back may also be rather accentuated.**

The front foot may land slightly wide, i.e. slightly to the off-side. This will be a deliberate modification of the Basic Action. The left shoulder will thus swing away a little earlier and the bowler will be more 'open-chested'. The bowling arm should be high, and at the moment of release the seam will be vertical and pointing slightly in the direction of the intended swing.

It is easier to swing the ball in if it is delivered from wide on the crease, rather than close to the stumps, but this presents less of a problem to the batsman, because of the angle of approach of the ball.

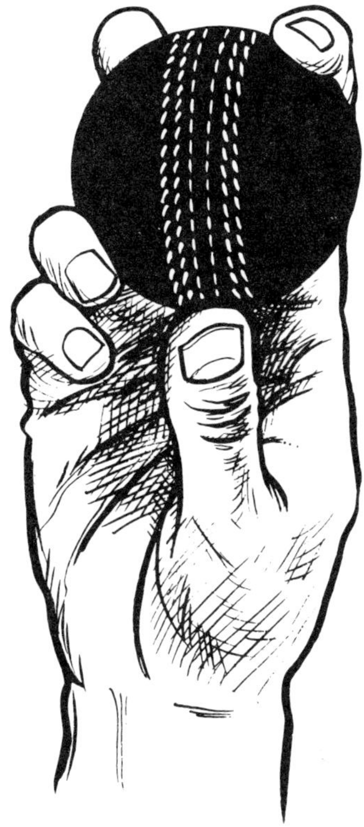

Fig. 4. Grip for in-swing

Use of in-swing

The bowler must normally aim to hit the wicket and to make the batsman play forward. If the batsman is on the front foot he may leave a gap between bat and pad, commonly called 'leaving the gate open', in which case a well pitched up ball which moves late may slip through. Further, since he is forced to play forward he will have less time to adjust his stroke and may well edge a catch to one of the close leg fieldsmen. A batsman playing forward finds it more difficult to judge the line of the ball accurately, as he has less time.

An occasional quicker in-swinger may cause the batsman to misjudge the length of the ball and playing back be out l.b.w.

Control of direction is of the utmost importance. Whilst a ball that swerves away wide of the stump may induce a false stroke, the ball that swings in and passes outside the batsman's legs is much less likely to do so. A mis-hit off such a ball is more likely to produce runs than a wicket, and, if it is missed, the wicket-keeper is set a problem.

CUTTERS

The off-cutter

The off-cutter is delivered with an action similar to that used to bowl an out-swinger, and can be used as a variation to it. The fingers pull across the seam at the instant of delivery, to impart spin, rather than being kept behind the ball as for the out-swinger.

The ball is gripped with the first two fingers which are close together and on top of the seam: the seam points straight or towards fine-leg: the thumb is directly opposite the fingers, under the seam, with the inside of the thumb pressed against it.

At the instant of delivery the first finger pulls down and across the seam whilst the hand rotates in a clockwise direction. This action can be strengthened if the bowling hand follows through across the body, to finish close to the left side as for the out-swinger.

The leg-cutter

The leg-cutter is used to describe a technique closely allied to that of the in-swinger, but by pulling the fingers across the seam of the ball at the moment of delivery, leg spin is imparted to the ball.

The ball is held between the first and second fingers, with the second finger pressing firmly on the outside edge of the seam and the first finger comfortably spaced from it on the smooth surface: the thumb is underneath and on the side of the seam (Fig. 5).

At the moment of delivery the second finger pulls down on the seam, the thumb pushes and the wrist rotates so that the palm of the hand faces outwards, thus causing the ball to spin from leg. The arm must be kept high in the delivery and there must be a full follow-through.

A variation is to hold the ball with a similar grip but with the fingers across the seam: the delivery is then closely akin to a fast leg-break.

To be effective, the leg-cutter must be bowled to a full length: the line of attack should be middle or middle and off stumps.

Fig. 5. Grip for leg-cutter

FAST BOWLING

It is probably true to say that most young cricketers want to bowl as fast as they can: it is a natural way of 'letting off steam', it is exhilarating to see the bails fly, and on the pitches upon which many of them play even moderate pace is likely to pose formidable problems to the young batsmen.

But as he moves into a higher class of cricket, and on to better pitches, he will find it a different story. **To a competent batsman, on a good wicket, nothing is more welcome than a bowler of less than top pace, who is inaccurate in length and direction.** His captain will also find it difficult to set a field capable of picking up chances, without giving away too many runs.

To be a successful fast bowler, the foundations must be there. **The fast bowler needs to be strong in the legs, and especially in the back.** He requires a high degree of fitness, stamina and suppleness. A certain aggressiveness of temper is an additional advantage, but none of these qualities can be used to the full unless the fast bowler has a good action.

On no account must a young fast bowler be allowed to 'over-bowl' either by striving for too much pace or bowling for too long. At each stage of his development normal pace should be that which he can sustain for several overs at a stretch. He should not be permitted to bowl for long periods of time, either in a match or in practice. Above all, a young fast bowler must be patient, acknowledging that only as he matures, and his strength and stamina increase, will he come to realize his full potential.

A fast bowler should warm-up before attempting to bowl at maximum pace. This is easily achieved at net practice, but **it also means that he must do so before taking the field in a match,** for he will usually be called upon to bowl the first over, and he needs to attack from the first ball. During the course of a game his captain should warn him when he is likely to be needed to bowl for another spell, and then he will be able to do some exercises to loosen-up.

The action

The principles laid down for the Basic Action (pages 29–37) are particularly vital for fast bowlers, for real pace demands perfect rhythm and timing, and these in turn depend upon harnessing every part of the body throughout the action. Perhaps more so than for any other type of bowler, the fast bowler's action starts at the moment he commences his run-up. The run-up must be one of gradual acceleration, with no check or stammer. It must lead to a gathering for the jump from the left foot. This jump into the 'coil' position must be such that it prevents the body weight from being transferred prematurely in the delivery. In trying for pace, many bowlers 'charge' up to the wicket, instead of building up steadily. A long run does not necessarily presume speed. It has often been said of a bowler that 'he runs faster than he bowls'.

The fast bowler must have a standard approach to the wicket, otherwise he will be prone to 'no-balling'. It is often useful to use check marks scratched on the ground, to establish a consistent stride: inconsistencies usually occur early in the run-up.

A powerful, rhythmical action, with a full swing of the bowling arm, will result in a pronounced follow-through. For this reason, if for no other, a fast bowler should bowl over the wicket, otherwise he will run on to the pitch in the follow-through.

Tactics

(*Note:* The following applies only to bowlers whose pace, relative to the batsman opposed to them, is unmistakenly fast. If it is only 'fastish', the tactics suggested for the medium-pace bowler are more relevant.)

The role of the fast bowler is essentially an attacking one. He is generally given the new ball and, therefore, needs to be able to swing the ball if he is to be really effective. If his action is good, he is more likely to make the ball swing away from the batsman, and occasionally bring one back off the pitch, but speed must always be his main weapon. The greater his pace and the faster the pitch, the greater is the bowler's margin of length and fast bowlers should vary their length more than others. A new batsman should be tested early in his innings by a 'yorker'; but a true yorker is a difficult ball to bowl, and one really well up to him, provided it is fast enough, has a good chance of getting through. Alternatively, at the start of his innings, an extra-fast ball, just short of a length, may find a batsman fatally late on his back stroke.

Then there is the genuinely short ball into which the bowler puts everything, in the hope that it may lift to an uncomfortable height, the 'bouncer'. If bowled occasionally, the 'bouncer' is a perfectly legitimate test of a batsman's morale and technique. A timid batsman is likely to flinch from it and edge it: a braver player may try to hook, mistime the stroke, and get caught. To be effective the 'bouncer' must be really fast, and so must the pitch.

If called upon to bowl on a dead pitch the fast bowler must virtually cut out the short ball and try to make the batsman play forward. **He must always bowl straight enough to make the batsman play and for this reason he must have a deep fine-leg,** since a snick on the leg-side would otherwise mean 'four'.

When the wicket is really helping him, he must refrain from experimenting and bowl straight and to a full length. By so doing he will give the ball more 'room' to do things 'in the air': it is bound to 'do things' off the pitch.

The positioning of his slips and gully is most important. The faster and livelier the pitch, the deeper they must be: their criterion must be the probable 'carry' of a snick off a good length ball. Slips also tend to stand too close to one another (*see* page 15).

Field Diagram A

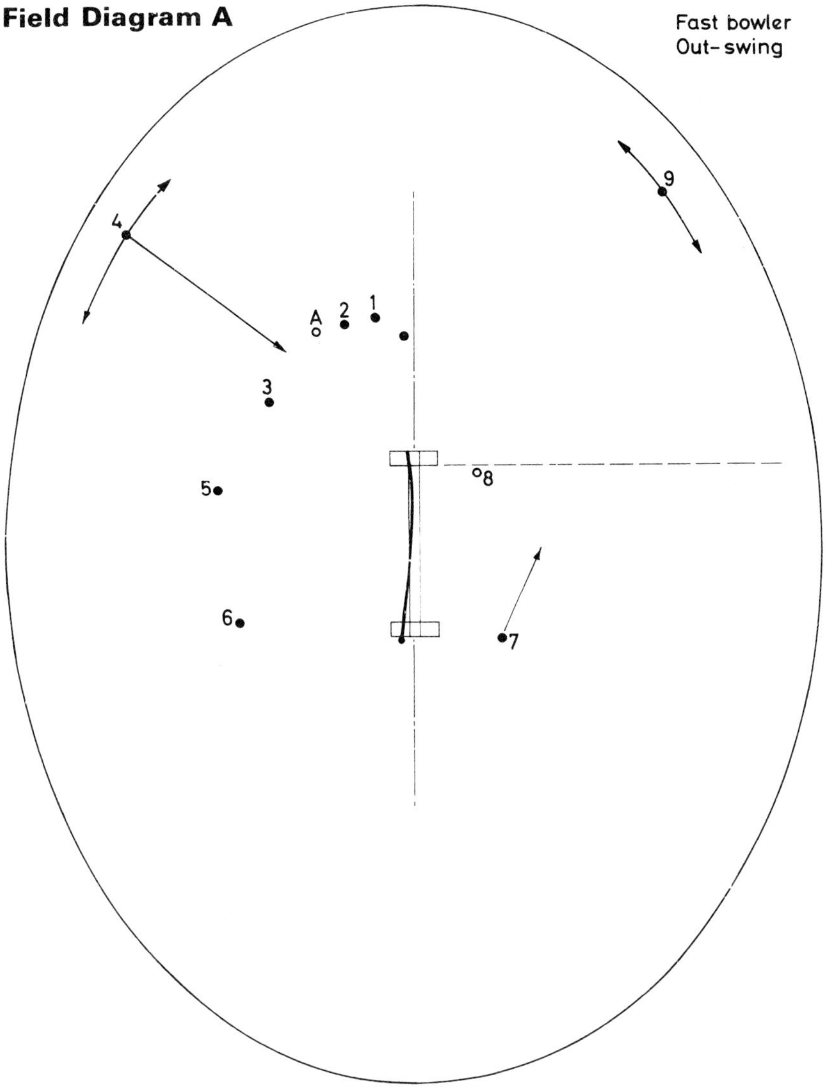

6/7 on off-side
1 First-slip
2 Second-slip
3 Gully
4 Third-man
5 Cover
6 Mid-off

3/2 on on-side
7 Mid-on
8 Square-leg
9 Long-leg

When the ball is swinging considerably No. 8 may move to third-slip (A), in which case No. 7 will be wider to cut off singles on the leg-side.

The fast bowler must be the complete master of himself, whether things are going well or ill. **When things are going well he must avoid getting over-excited, for, if he does, he may start to rush up to the wicket, try to bowl too fast, and thus lose rhythm and with it that vital length and direction.** If, on the other hand, things go against him, he must equally keep his head, and at the same time, harden his heart. **It is probably more true of a fast bowler than of any other, that in the long run the man who never gives up trying will have most success.**

It must be emphasized that any slight deficiencies in the footwear of the fast bowler, either the comfort of his boots, or the grip of his spikes, will lessen or even nullify his efficiency. The fast bowler must have strong, comfortable and well-spiked boots; his socks must be thick and preferably without darns. Any imperfections will become abrasive during the course of a long day in the field; blisters and bruises take much longer to heal than to acquire.

This section began with a word on the fitness and physique needed by the fast bowler; such attributes seldom come by chance and so the fast bowler must be prepared to work hard to establish the high standards of fitness required for this most physically demanding of cricket roles. Such work should be done out of season, but is especially important immediately prior to the start of a season.

MEDIUM-PACE BOWLING

In all classes of cricket, medium-paced bowlers tend to predominate, as they can be used on any type of pitch. They can be deadly under favourable conditions and yet, when the wicket is plumb or when the batting side is chasing runs, invaluable in pinning the batsman down by bowling a good line and length to a well-placed field. Above all, the medium-paced bowler needs accuracy. **If pace and fire are the great virtues for a fast bowler, and spin and cunning for a slow bowler, it is for this accuracy that the medium-paced bowler is asked above everything.**

But uniform accuracy of length and direction, though it may be effective enough on bad wickets, or against unskilful batsmen, will not alone prove effective against good batsmen on good wickets. A medium-paced bowler must therefore try to learn to swing or spin the ball: seldom should he attempt leg-breaks. Some great bowlers have been able to 'cut' the ball from leg to off (*see* page 44): on the other hand, many medium-paced bowlers are able to 'cut' the ball from off to leg (*see* pages 43–44).

The ability to deceive a batsman by change of pace is particularly valuable because it is independent of the state of the pitch. Change of pace may make the batsman play the wrong stroke, or mistime the correct stroke. He may have met three good-length balls securely by a correctly played forward

Field Diagram B

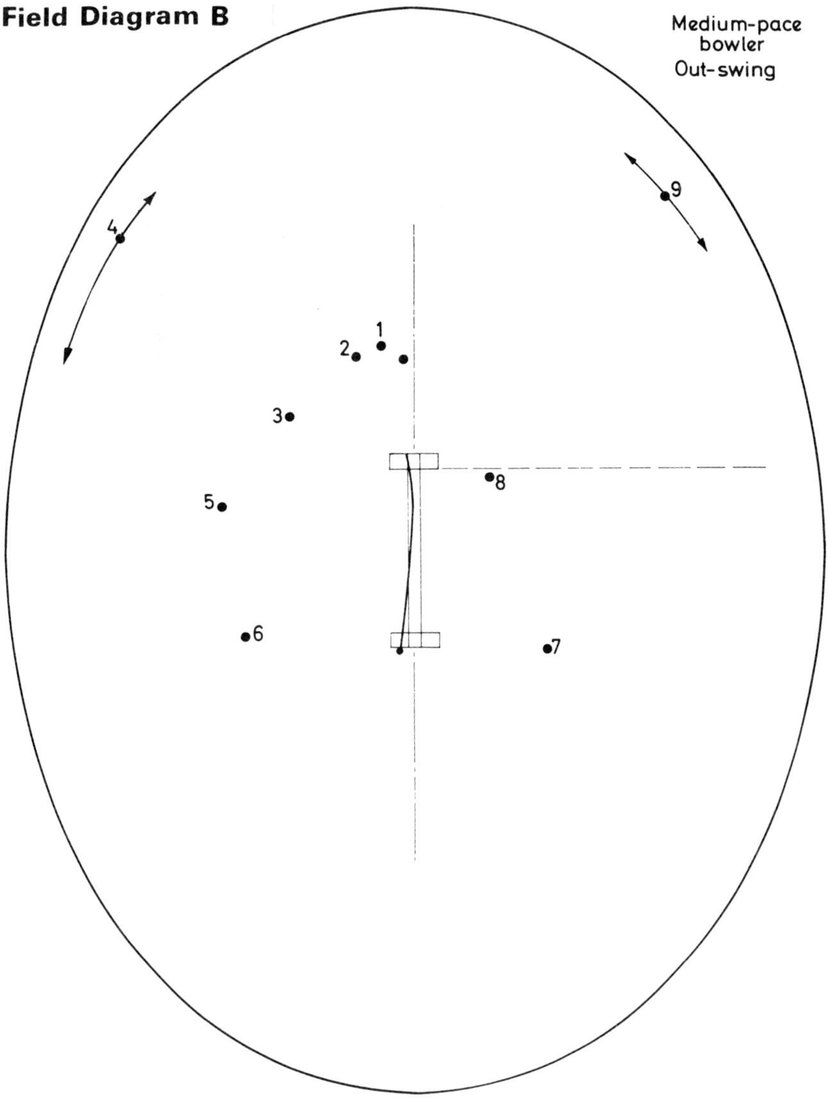

6 on off-side
1 First-slip
2 Second-slip
3 Gully
4 Third-man
5 Cover
6 Mid-off

3 on on-side
7 Mid-on
8 Square-leg
9 Long-leg

Field Diagram C

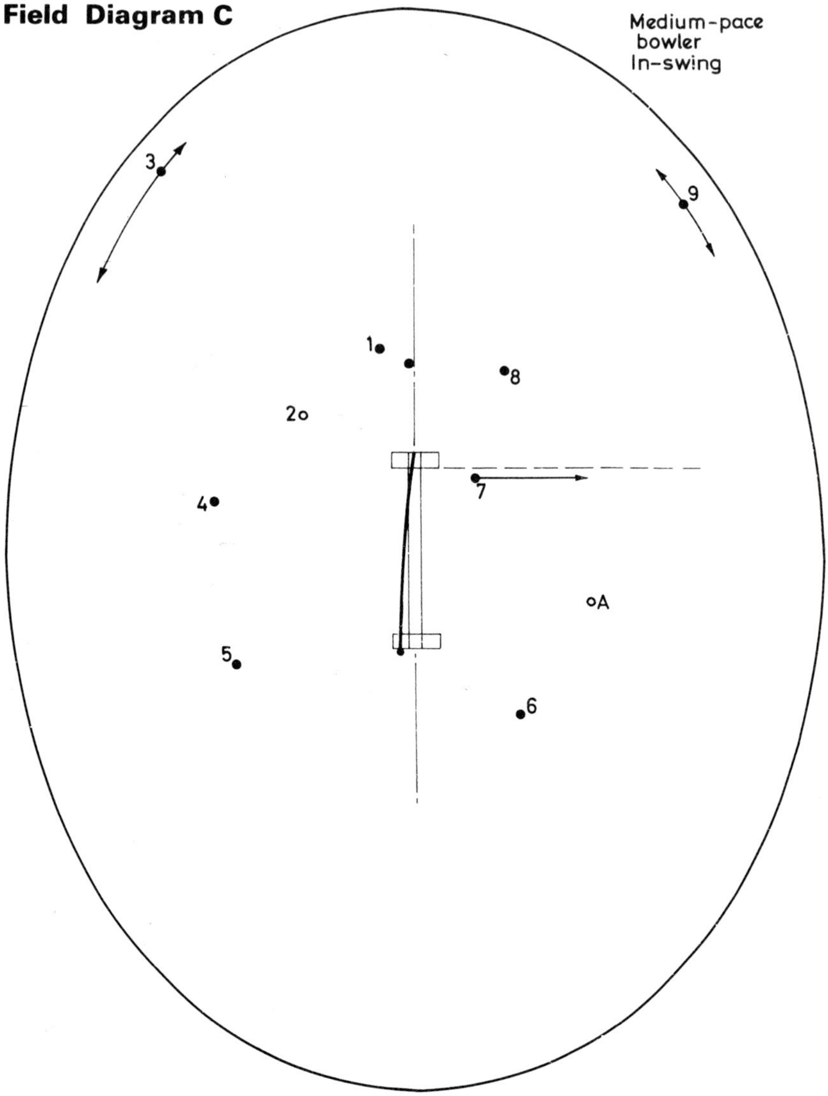

5/4 on off-side
1 Slip
2 Gully
3 Third-man
4 Cover
5 Mid-off

4/5 on on-side
6 Mid-on
7 Square-leg
8 Leg-slip
9 Long-leg

Some bowlers may prefer to have No. 2 on the leg-side (A). When there is little swing No. 7 will drop back to save the single.

Field Diagram D

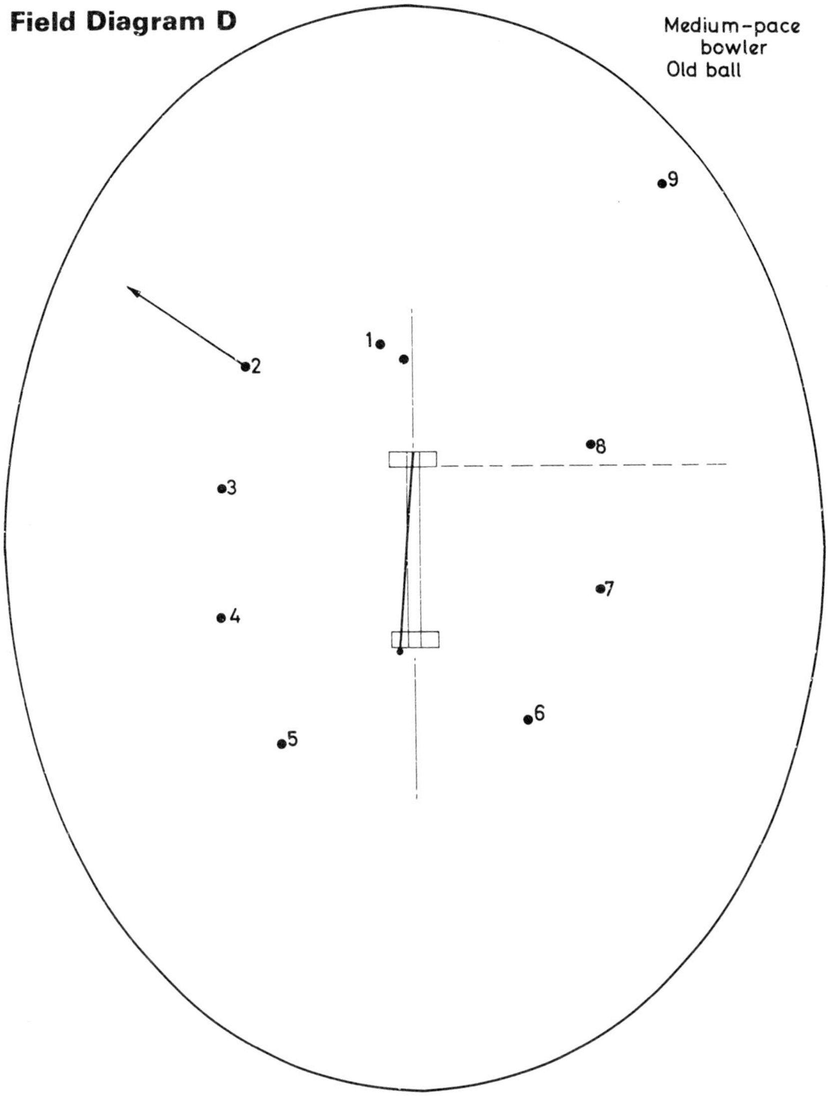

5 on off-side
1 Slip
2 Short-third-man
3 Cover
4 Extra-cover
5 Mid-off

4 on on-side
6 Mid-on
7 Mid-wicket
8 Square-leg
9 Long-leg

stroke, but if a fourth ball of the same length is bowled a little slower, the same forward stroke may lead to a catch in front of the wicket. Similarly, after a series of balls of uniform length, a ball bowled a little faster may catch the batsman unawares. Such changes of pace must not be so pronounced as to 'signal' themselves to the batsman, by alteration of run-up and delivery.

The bowler must learn to alter the angle of his delivery to the batsman by making full use of the width of the crease, i.e. bowling one ball from close to the wicket and another from just inside the return crease. Such variation may cause the batsman to play down the 'wrong line'. These are the resources of the medium-paced bowler. Unless the score board, the clock, or perhaps the captain, dictate defensive strategy, he, like every other type of bowler, must attack the batsman. For the medium-paced bowler, attacking means bowling at the wicket, making the batsman play every ball.

The state of the pitch will influence him. If the pitch is easy-paced he will rely mainly on swing or change of pace: he may also have to push the ball through a little faster or a little further up than usual, in order to make the batsman play forward, or at least prevent him from playing back in comfort. On a pitch which is receptive, he may be able to spin or 'cut' the ball, supported by fielders in close catching positions.

He must always be prepared to make adjustments in his field according to the nature of the pitch and the type of batsman to whom he is bowling. Until absolutely forced to do so such changes must be made on the basis of attack and not defence.

Sometimes he will be forced, by the state of the game, to bowl defensively. It is then that control of direction, as well as length, is so essential. In first-class cricket, many bowlers tend to direct their defensive bowling at 'middle and leg'. But this demands a very high degree of accuracy, and young bowlers would be far better advised to concentrate on the off stump, for very few of the batsmen opposed to them will have an effective answer; their mis-hits will be more likely to go to hand, and less likely to 'carry' for fours, than if made on the on-side. Such defensive bowling should be supported by an inner and outer ring of fieldsmen, the outer to stop the fours and the inner to save singles; for it must always be remembered that four singles an over represent a good run-rate.

The job of the medium-paced bowler demands just as much determination, just as much sustained concentration as that of the fast bowler, probably more, since he must expect to bowl in far longer spells. A flying start must not betray him into over-confidence and any relaxation: still less must he allow punishment to 'rattle' or depress him. There will be days when he cannot bowl as well as he knows he should be able to: others, though bowling well, nothing will go right for him. In either case, he must go on trying, remembering that, whereas for the batsman one ball can mean final eclipse, for him one ball can mean triumph.

LEFT-ARM SEAM BOWLING

The medium or faster left-arm bowler more often than not bowls over the wicket. From this angle, and directing his line of attack at the middle and off stumps, he is making the best of both worlds, and presenting the batsman with a double problem: for though his natural tendency will be to swing the ball in, the basic line of his trajectory will be from leg to off, and his swinging ball is less likely to finish wide of the leg stump, whilst the one that does not swing at all will be 'leaving the batsman' who may well play inside it.

The setting of the field for such a bowler must inevitably present a problem. As long as the ball is really moving in the air, he will have an attacking field, inevitably to some extent split between the off and on sides. But if the ball is not moving much, or if the batsman seems to be getting on top and finding gaps in the field, he must make up his mind how he means to bowl, i.e. primarily 'inwards' at the wicket, or 'outwards' at and outside the off stump, and then must set his field accordingly.

SPIN BOWLING

This section is entitled 'Spin Bowling' rather than 'Slow Bowling' on the principle that most slow bowlers regard, and must regard, spin as the primary weapon of their attack. They must, of course, also hope to deceive the batsman in the air: to do so they must bowl slow enough to set him something of a problem in gauging the 'arc' of their flight, but not so slow that he can readily move out to the pitch of the ball and kill the break, or play it comfortably off the back foot if he stays at home. If, on the other hand, they try to bowl too fast they will lose this asset and very likely their length as well. In time, experience will teach them what pace suits their particular type of bowling best, how to vary this normal pace and, better still, how to 'flight' the ball in the true sense of the word; they must also aim to develop tactical skill.

There have been a few great slow bowlers who did not spin the ball very much; perhaps they did not need to, such was their mastery of length, flight and tactical cunning. **But for most slow bowlers real power of spin is essential to success, and once a boy has made up his mind to become a spin bowler, he must never rest until he has acquired it.**

Like all other bowlers he must be grounded in the principles of the Basic Action, for by these alone can he hope to command control, whilst the proper use of his body in the delivery is a powerful reinforcement to spin. **But if the ball is to be really spun, the fingers and the wrist must do it and a boy must start learning how to make them do it at a very early stage.**

The mechanics of off- and leg-spin are analysed in the sections below devoted to these types of bowling. As soon as a bowler has been grounded in the Basic Action he should be encouraged to experiment with and practise spin. He should begin to do this at quite short range and perhaps underhand, gradually raising the height of his arm in delivery and increasing the range up to the length at which, according to his age, he will have to bowl in a match. He may start this practice with any sort of ball, provided that it is not too big and he can grip it properly: so long as the surface is true, the more responsive it is to spin, the better, for this will encourage him.

Sooner or later the coach must help him to decide whether he has the strength of finger, the flexibility of wrist and, perhaps, the imagination to warrant committing himself to the role of the genuine spin bowler. If he so decides, **he must intensify his practice of spin and do everything he can to strengthen his fingers: even by himself he can do much by the constant squeezing and 'flipping' of any rubber ball.**

He must also decide whether he is going to be an off-spinner or a leg-spinner. He will be very unwise to try to combine the two, for, if he is really to spin the ball, it is extremely difficult to bowl both breaks and at the same time to maintain consistency of action and therefore of length: but an even stronger reason is that it is impossible to set a satisfactory attacking field for both.

The final choice should be based on the 'natural' bowling action of the boy and on his personal preference. Many youngsters bowl leg-breaks more 'naturally' than off-breaks. But at a later stage off-spin is easier to combine with control of length and direction. However, the general technique of the off-spin bowler is so closely allied with that of the medium-pace bowler, that a boy who begins as the latter, may, at a later stage, switch over to off-spin without any readjustment. This is not true of the leg-break bowler, for whom a considerable readjustment is necessary before he can bowl in any other style.

But if off-spin may seem to be the safer bet, leg-spin may offer the greater prize. Though it is harder to bowl accurately, it operates more viciously and most batsmen are more fallible to it. This is particularly true of school cricket where a leg-spin bowler of any merit is worth his weight in gold; few school batsmen play leg-break bowling convincingly, many commit early suicide to them, some are out to them almost before they go in. Nor is success in school cricket the highest prize to be won: records show the decisive part often played by leg-spin bowlers in club cricket and in international cricket.

Why then, do so few boys continue bowling leg-breaks as they mature? Perhaps they are discouraged by the difficulties in control; more probably they are discouraged by the lack of opportunity to bowl in a match.

The introduction of 'limited overs' cricket at all levels of the game has unfortunately led to fewer opportunities for spin bowlers of all kinds, and

Abdul Qadir. One of the few modern leg-spin bowlers: note arm high and wrist cocked at the moment of delivery *Patrick Eagar*

Ray Illingworth. Everything correct for the off-spinner *Patrick Eagar*

John Emburey. At the moment of release, the left leg is braced, the arm high and the ball is being released as the hand is level with the head *Patrick Eagar*

Jim Laker. Legendary for his nineteen wickets v Australia at Old Trafford in 1956, this famous photograph is a model for off-spinners *The Photo Source/Central Press*

particularly for leg-spinners. It would be regrettable if this tendency were to continue to such an extent that a coach felt obliged to advise young spin bowlers to specialize in a different department of the game, in order to have a better chance of participating.

It is often laid down as a cardinal rule that a bowler must first concentrate on learning to bowl a length before he starts practising spin or swerve. Whilst it is certainly true that a bowler ultimately must have a good command of length and direction, a modern view is that a boy must concentrate first on learning to really spin the ball, and then learn to control the length and direction. This view is supported by the argument that to bowl spin, especially leg-spin, demands adjustments to the Basic Action, and these adjustments cannot easily be made once an action has become established. It is perhaps significant that some of the greatest spin bowlers admit to having practised their spin long and intensively before attempting to bowl in a match.

LEG-SPIN: GOOGLY: TOP-SPIN

The googly and top-spinner are really developments of the leg-spinner and are complementary to it. Leg-spin and top-spin are self-explanatory. The googly is a ball which, for reasons explained below, turns from the off: its value to the leg-break bowler is that, being bowled with only minor adjustments in his action, it may deceive the batsman.

A young bowler should be strongly discouraged from over-bowling the googly since it involves considerable strain on the shoulder and arm muscles. But it is a difficult ball to control and he must therefore practise it sufficiently to gain the necessary accuracy. There is, however, a real danger that, if he becomes 'bitten' with the googly, the adjustments to his action, small though they may be, will become a habit and he will eventually find he is unable to spin his leg-break: he will then have exchanged his most dangerous ball for another which, except for the element of surprise, is easier to play. Even one or two international bowlers have had this unfortunate experience.

For all three deliveries the grip is the same: it is the action of the wrist which is different.

The grip

The ball is 'bedded down' in the first three fingers, which are spaced comfortably apart. The first two lie across the seam, the top joints taking most of the pressure: the third and little fingers are curled below them, so that the top joint of the third finger, lying across the seam, presses hard upwards against it. This third finger is the main lever for the spin: the base of the thumb rests lightly on the seam, and takes no part in the spinning of the ball.

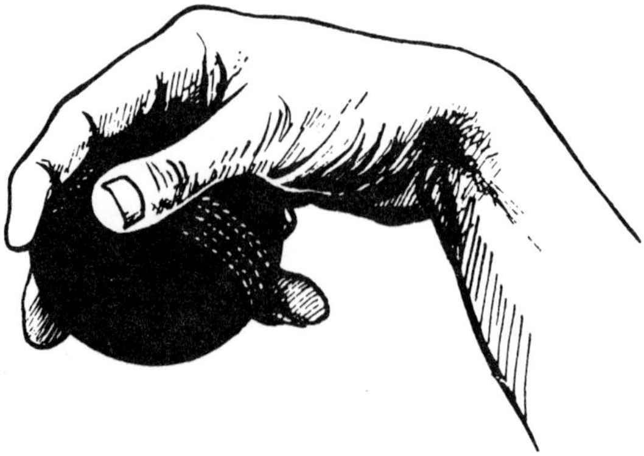

Fig. 6. Grip for leg-spin: as seen by the batsman

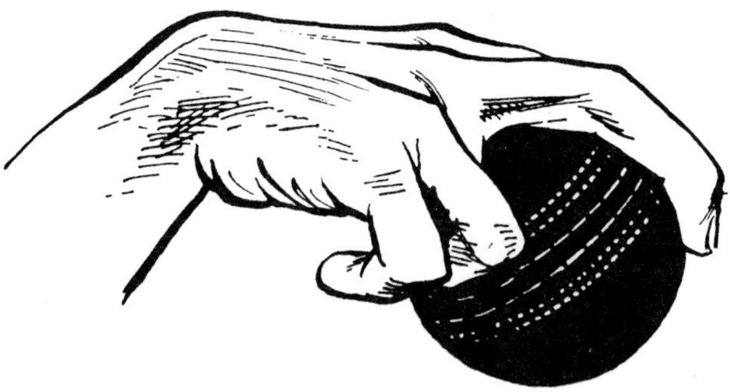

Fig. 7. Grip for leg-spin: as seen from behind the bowler

The wrist

(*a*) *For the leg-break*

The wrist will be bent forward as far as possible until the moment of release (Fig. 8) **and, as the arm swings over, the palm of the hand will be facing the batsman or even fine-leg. The wrist now flips towards the batsman rotating in an anti-clockwise direction and, as the ball is delivered, the third finger flicks outwards and forwards. The hand will follow through across the body:** the fingers will be stretched and the palm facing downwards (Fig. 9).

(*b*) *For the googly*

The wrist leads and rotates earlier and further than for the leg-break, so that at the moment of release the back of the hand is facing the batsman: the ball now comes out of the hand over the top of the third and little fingers thus imparting off-spin (Fig. 10).

To help this rotation of the wrist the left foot may land a little wider, i.e. further to the off side: this will allow the essential dipping of the left shoulder which in turn will result in the bowling arm pointing down the pitch in the follow-through: at the finish, the palm of the hand will face square-leg.

The easiest way to acquire the 'feel' of the googly is to bowl it under-hand.

(*c*) *For the top-spinner*

The forward flip of the wrist begins just a little earlier than for the leg-break so that the spin imparted to the ball by the flick of the third finger is directly down the line of the flight and not towards the slips: at the moment of release the palm of the hand will be facing mid-on: at the finish the arm and hand will be straight down the wicket. Few bowlers have been able to bowl a top-spinner at will: it usually results from the wrist rotating too much for the leg-break or too little for the googly.

The action

As for all other types of bowler, a regular and rhythmic run-up, which will bring him well balanced to the crease, is essential.

A good pivot of the body in the delivery is of the first importance for it will reinforce the flip of the wrist and the action of the fingers, and will add to the ball's spin and pace off the pitch.

As the arm starts to swing up into the delivery it must be fully extended, even locked at the elbow: if it is not, the bowler is unlikely to command accuracy.

The higher the action the better the control of direction, and the greater the bounce off the pitch.

TACTICS FOR THE LEG-SPIN BOWLER

Very few leg-break bowlers have sufficient command of length and direction to justify their captain ever using them defensively: for such defensive bowling the medium-pace, or off-spin bowler is the natural choice. **The role of the leg-spinner is essentially to attack.**

Fig. 8. Leg-spin: moment of delivery

Fig. 9. Leg-spin: follow-through

Fig. 10. Googly: just after release

Fig. 11. Googly: follow-through

Almost without exception he should bowl over the wicket, for if he bowls 'round', the leg-break that pitches straight is likely to miss the stumps and, under the Laws, he cannot get an l.b.w. decision from any ball that pitches outside the leg stump.

He must bowl at the stumps; his exact line will vary according to the degree of turn. He must keep the ball up, for a delivery that can be comfortably watched from the pitch and played off the back foot, is no use however much it turns.

His field must be stationed accordingly: this means that his in-fielders must be close enough to prevent singles, for otherwise he cannot hope to attack any batsmen with a planned sequence of balls. On the other hand, he must be prepared to invite the batsman to play strokes, indeed he

Field Diagram E

Leg-spin bowler
True pitch

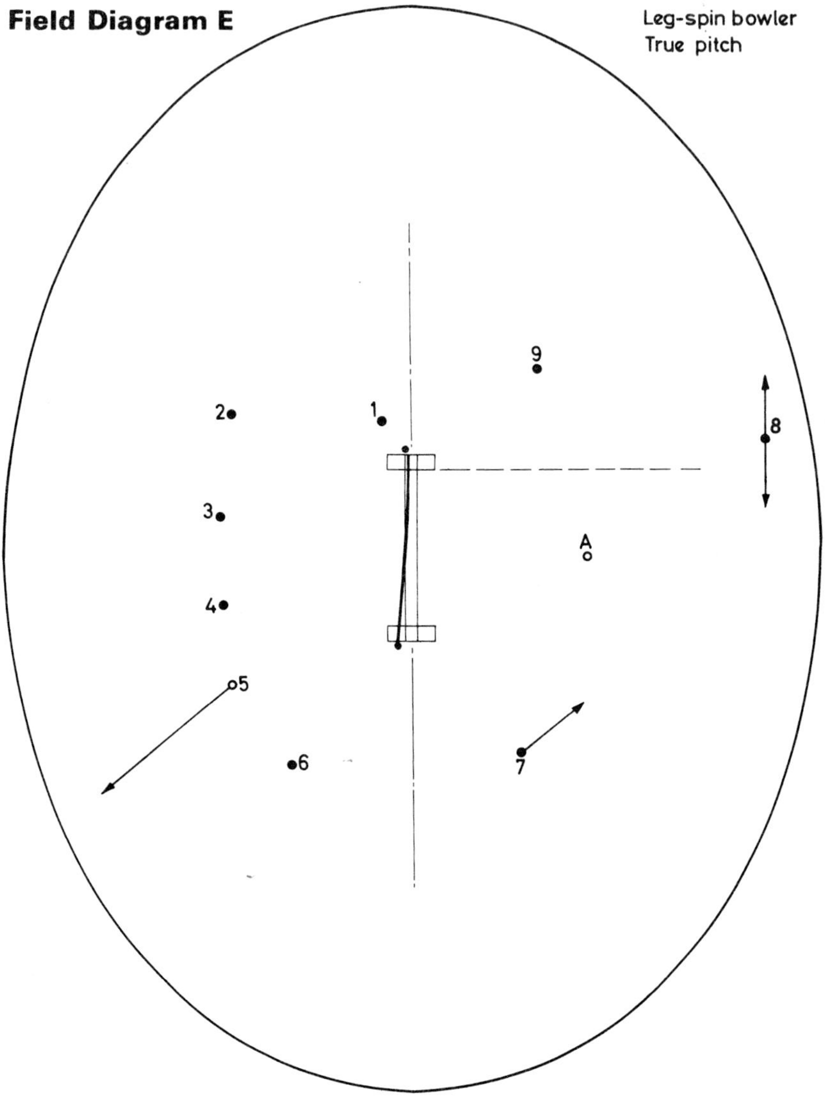

6/5 on off-side
1 Slip
2 Short-third-man
3 Cover
4 Extra-cover
5 Deep-extra-cover
6 Mid-off

3/4 on on-side
7 Mid-on
8 Deep-square-leg
9 Short-fine-leg

An extra fielder may be needed at mid-wicket (A) instead of No. 5 depending on the batsman or the accuracy of the bowler.

Field Diagram F

Leg-spin bowler
Turning pitch

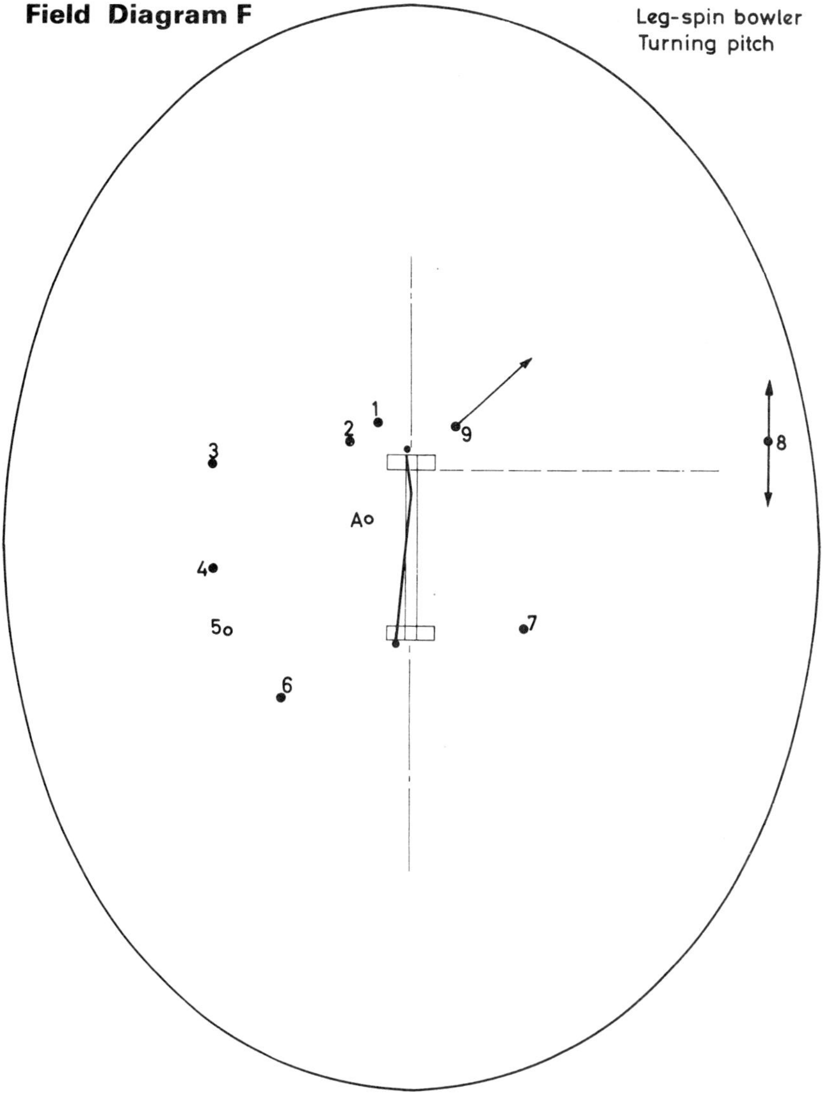

6 on off-side
1 First-slip
2 Second-slip
3 Short-third-man
4 Cover
5 Extra-cover
6 Mid-off

3 on on-side
7 Mid-on
8 Deep-square-leg
9 Leg-slip

Against a defensive batsman the bowler may prefer a silly-mid-off (A) instead of No. 5.

should want him to do so, and to do this with confidence he must have some fielders deep enough to save fours. He must recognize that one of his best chances of getting a wicket is from the ball which spins away to the off-side and is mis-hit into the covers: these fielders, therefore, must not be too deep. He should try to dispense with wide long-on and by leaving that inviting gap tempt the batsman to hit against the spin. He would not be human if he did not sometimes bowl a long-hop and sometimes drop the ball on or outside the batsman's leg stump: he must, therefore, also have a deep-square-leg.

The faster and truer the pitch, the more he must try to 'give the ball room in the air', and to deceive the batsman by slight changes of pace and flight or by enticing him to chase the ball wide on the off. If the state of the game allows he must be prepared to experiment even at the cost of runs.

The deader the pitch, the more he must 'push the ball through' at the batsman, i.e. bowl a little faster, and not allow him to play it off the back foot.

On a really difficult pitch accuracy is everything: he must concentrate on length and direction, and his normal spin and the wicket should do the rest.

If he can bowl a googly, he should bowl it early on at each new batsman, for, if it does not dismiss him, it will start him looking for another which in fact may be a leg-break; but he should use it sparingly, for to bowl it too often may defeat its object and in doing so he may well lose his length for the leg-break: moreover, his field cannot be set for both. The most promising target for the googly is the batsman who likes to push forward defensively and tends to 'leave the gate open' when he does so, or the back player who looks as if he does not know which way the ball is turning.

If the bowler can command the top-spinner it is particularly valuable on wickets off which the ball is turning sharply and against a batsman who is concentrating on back play.

Of all bowlers, he has most need of an alert mind and an equable temperament. He must realize that because he is a leg-spinner he is liable at times to be inaccurate and expensive. **He must take the rough with the smooth, he must never mind being hit, he must never get rattled or give up trying, reminding himself that, if his is the most difficult of all bowling crafts, it is also perhaps the most intriguing, the most exciting and the most rewarding.**

OFF-SPIN

Off-spin bowlers are in a sense stock bowlers in that they can be used on all types of pitch: they can bowl defensively when required, and in attack when conditions suit them. They vary, of course, in pace but most of them find that to make the ball bite on good wickets they must bowl well below medium pace. It is with this type of bowler that this section is concerned.

The grip

The grip described is that for an adult and some modifications may be needed for a young bowler with a smaller hand. Whilst long strong fingers are, of course, an asset for a 'finger spinner', even a boy with a hand slightly smaller than normal should not feel that he cannot spin the ball adequately, or that what is written here of the grip is impracticable for him.

The first finger is the main spinning finger, and is helped by the middle finger: the top joint of the first finger is pressed hard along and against the seam which runs at right-angles to the forearm: the middle finger is on top of the seam. The further these first two fingers can with comfort be spaced apart, the greater the leverage they can apply: the degree of the spin can, in fact, be altered by varying the spacing of them. The other two fingers, curled under the ball, help to hold it in position: the base of the thumb rests lightly on the side of the ball. As in the bowling of leg-breaks the thumb takes no part in the spinning of the ball (Fig. 12).

Fig. 12. Grip for off-spin

The ball must not be 'bedded down' in the palm of the hand since it is with the top joints that maximum spin can be imparted.

An alternative grip, especially useful for a bowler with a smaller hand who cannot achieve a wide separation of the first two fingers, is to place the first finger against the inside edge of the seam, which runs in the direction of the forearm: at the moment of release the first finger can then exert pressure against the seam.

For an off-break the ball must be spun clockwise, i.e. from left to right, and the action of the hand is much the same as turning the knob to open a door: the wrist will turn outwards and, as it does so, the first two fingers, and especially the first, will straighten. As the wrist turns the hand flips forwards and downwards, finishing with the palm upwards.

Fig. 13. Off-break: just after release

The action

The adjustments which may be made in the Basic Action to increase off-spin are slight but definite. **The wrist should be fully cocked before it begins its upward swing: the palm will thus face directly upwards. The left foot in the delivery stride should be taken slightly across the line of delivery: i.e. to the on-side: this will follow if the initial sideways turn of the body has been accentuated. The delivery stride should be rather shorter, so that the ball can be delivered from maximum height. During the delivery the bowler should be rotating more around the front leg and braced side, than any other type of bowler. He must have the feeling that the bowling arm swings over late and across the body, so that the fingers 'drag down' the side of the ball as it is released. The head must be kept up and the ball released as the hand is level with it.**

The 'floater'

This, as the name suggests, is a ball which drifts away from the batsman in the air. It is a useful variation which most of the experienced off-spinners command. In the grip most commonly used the first and second fingers are separated as for the off-spinner, but the first finger is extended along the seam rather than being bent back at right-angles to it. The thumb is close to the first finger and is pressed against the side of the ball: the fourth and little fingers rest lightly under the ball.

The action is similar to that for an off-spinner, but the hand works quite differently. At the instant of delivery the wrist should be firmly behind the ball and the seam vertical, exactly as for the normal out-swinger, and the bowler should feel that the ball is being pushed towards slip by the first finger and thumb. There will be no rotation of the wrist.

TACTICS OF THE OFF-SPINNER

An off-spin bowler will normally bowl over the wicket to a right-handed batsman on a good wicket: on the other hand, when bowling to a left-handed batsman or when the ball is turning, he will generally bowl round the wicket.

He should, therefore, spend as much time during practice bowling round as over the wicket so that he will acquire the ability to bowl to whatever line of attack he may be required to use.

Only when the ball is turning will he be justified in bowling to a close leg-side field as only then will the ball be likely to be edged to them: further, unless he can command real accuracy of length and direction, the close fieldsmen will be exposed to the risk of serious injury.

The bowler should, under normal conditions, direct his line of attack at the off stump and set his field accordingly, thus forcing the batsman to take risks if he tries to avoid the arc covered by the fielders. He will hope to wear the batsman down by accuracy or deceive him by a change of pace, by flight, or with the 'floater'.

The object of change of pace, of which something has been said in the section on medium-pace bowling, is to deceive the batsman as to when the ball will reach him; by flight, the bowler is out to delude him as to where it will pitch, in other words to make the ball look as if it will drop further up to him than in fact it will.

There are several methods of 'flighting' the ball. One is to deliver the ball at normal pace, but with a slightly higher trajectory, from two or three feet behind the bowling crease. Another, and probably the most effective method, is to release the ball rather earlier, i.e. just before the hand reaches the vertical, but at the same time ensuring the arm goes through at the normal pace. The bowler must experiment to discover which of these or other suggestions are effective for him: he must also realize that to master this difficult art of 'flight' needs hard work and constant practice.

In general it may be said that the better the pitch, the more the bowler must rely on beating the batsman in the air rather than off the ground: to do this he will tend to bowl a little slower than his normal pace.

Should he find himself compelled to bowl defensively he will either bowl wider, with a corresponding adjustment of his field, or, if he is accurate, bowl a little quicker and attack the middle and leg stump, also with corresponding adjustment of his field.

It is when the ball is turning sharply that the off-spinner comes into his own. His spin will now really bite and the ball will at times also 'stop' and 'lift'. **Under these conditions he will bowl round the wicket and so greatly increase his chance of getting a batsman l.b.w., for an off-break which bowled over the wicket would miss the stumps can, if bowled round the wicket, hit them.**

Field Diagram G

Off-spin bowler
True pitch

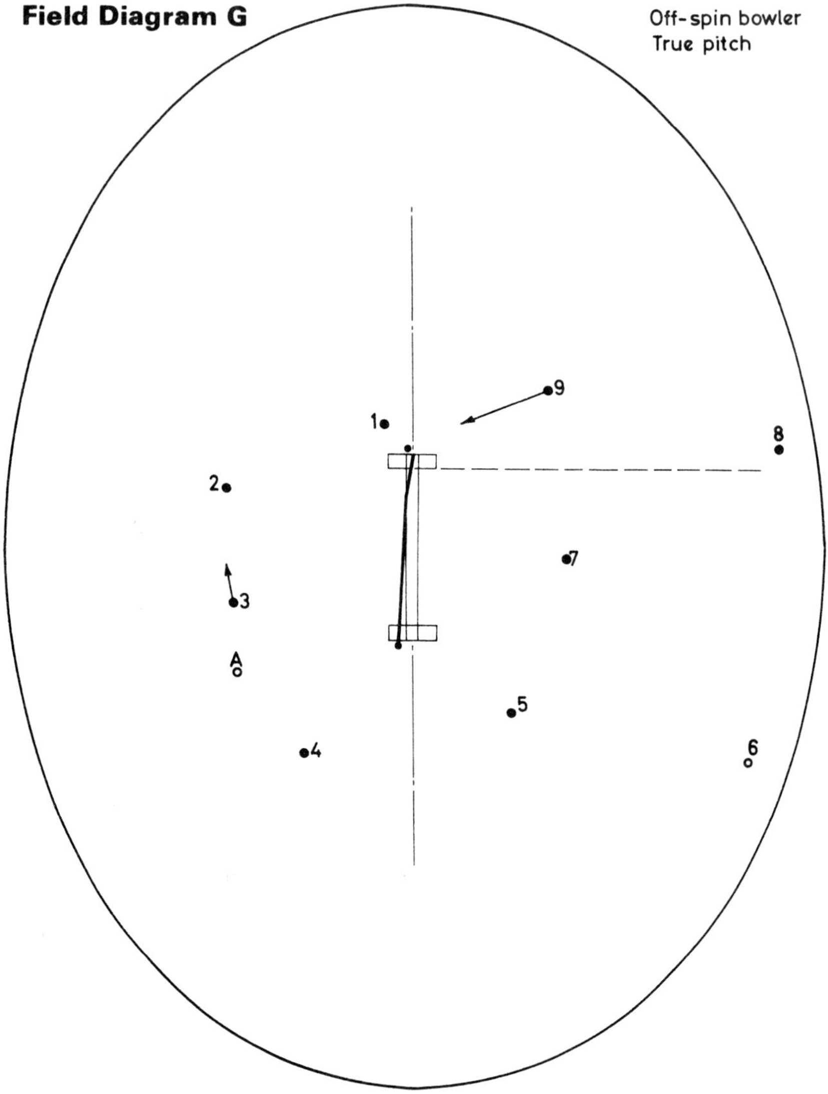

4/5 on off-side
1 Slip
2 Cover-point
3 Extra-cover
4 Mid-off

5/4 on on-side
5 Mid-on
6 Deep-mid-wicket
7 Mid-wicket
8 Deep-square-leg
9 Fine-leg

An extra fielder may be needed on the off-side (A) instead of No. 6 depending on the bowler's line of attack and on the batsman.

Field Diagram H

Off-spin bowler
Turning pitch

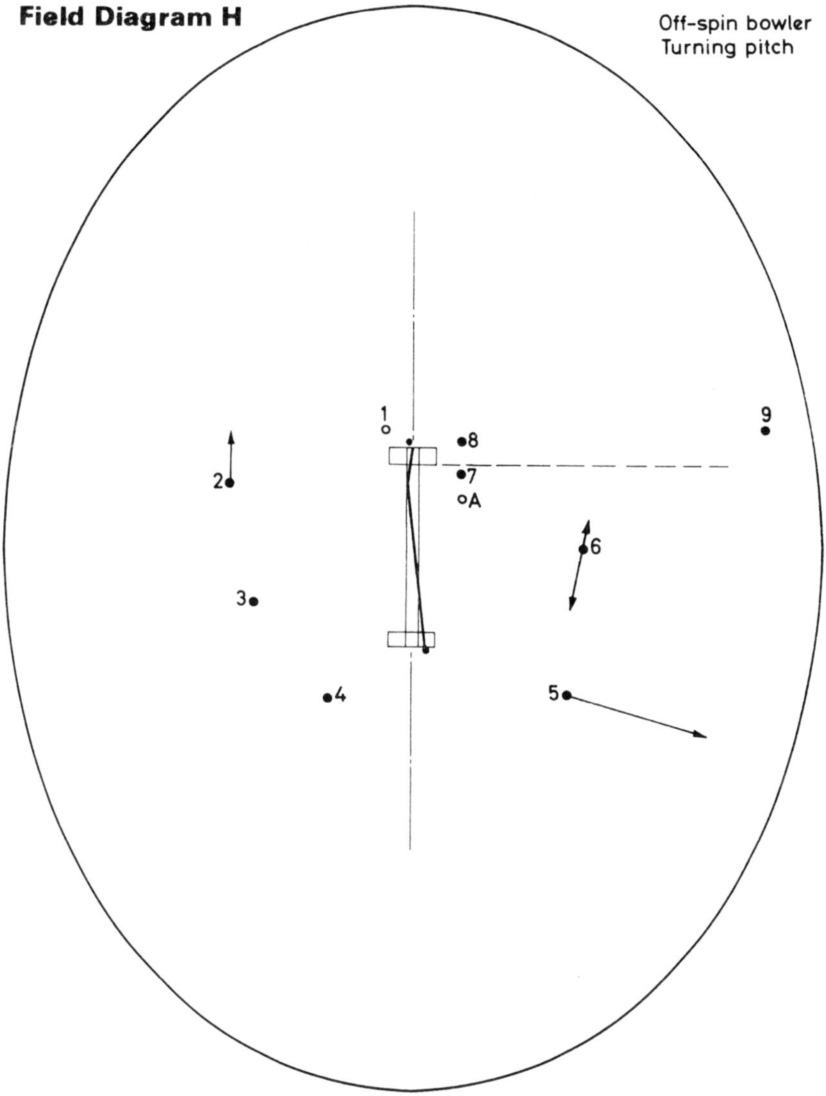

4/3 on off-side
1 Slip
2 Cover-point
3 Extra-cover
4 Mid-off

5/6 on on-side
5 Mid-on
6 Mid-wicket
7 Short-leg
8 Short-leg
9 Deep-square-leg

An extra fielder may be needed on the leg-side (A) instead of No. 1 depending on the degree of turn and on the batsman.

The arc of his field will now be different and concentrated more on the leg-side: but he should still bowl at the off stump, remembering that the more the pitch is taking spin the more likely it is that a ball which pitches straight will miss the wicket.

He should bowl slightly faster than on a true pitch and his aim will be to bring the batsman on to the front foot. Accuracy is vitally important; if he intersperses good length balls with long-hops and full-tosses, his fielders will not have the confidence to stand close enough to the bat to take chance catches from defensive strokes. He must make the batsman play: balls which are on or outside his legs can be ignored or attacked with a cross bat. To sustain this accuracy the less experienced bowlers must resist the temptation to bowl too fast or to spin the ball too much.

The slower the pitch the fuller length he must bowl. If the pitch is muddy he must constantly clean the ball and especially its seam.

LEFT-HAND SPIN BOWLING

The classical left-hander is the slow bowler who spins the ball from leg. He must also rely on flight and change of pace.

The basic principles governing his action, his grip and method of imparting spin, are exactly similar to those of the off-spin bowler.

Almost without exception he will bowl round the wicket to a right-hand batsman. Whilst in common with other types of bowler he should make use of the width of the crease from time to time, **his normal delivery will be from close to the stumps.**

When bowling to a left-hand batsman he will bowl over the wicket, only going round when he can turn the ball sharply. To the left-hander he is an off-spin bowler and his tactics and line of attack will be the same as those of an off-spinner bowling to a right-hand batsman.

On good true wickets he cannot expect to turn the ball as much as a 'wrist' spinner, but he should be far more accurate. His line of attack will be at or just outside the off-stump, with a predominantly off-side field.

Like every other bowler he will hope to attack, but at times he will be forced to bowl defensively with an inner and outer ring of fielders: the former to inhibit short singles, the latter to cut off the fours. He must be prepared, if the conditions of the game allow, to 'buy' wickets, tempting the batsman to drive. If he is getting little help from the pitch, it is even more important that he should deliver the ball from close to the stumps.

It is when the ball is really turning that such a bowler should hope to prove a match winner. He will now attack the middle stump, concentrating on length and his natural spin, and keeping the ball well up. Ideally he should be able to bowl to a silly-mid-off, a gully and a slip. As always, he must regard his field as elastic and be prepared, but only if so forced by the

Field Diagram I

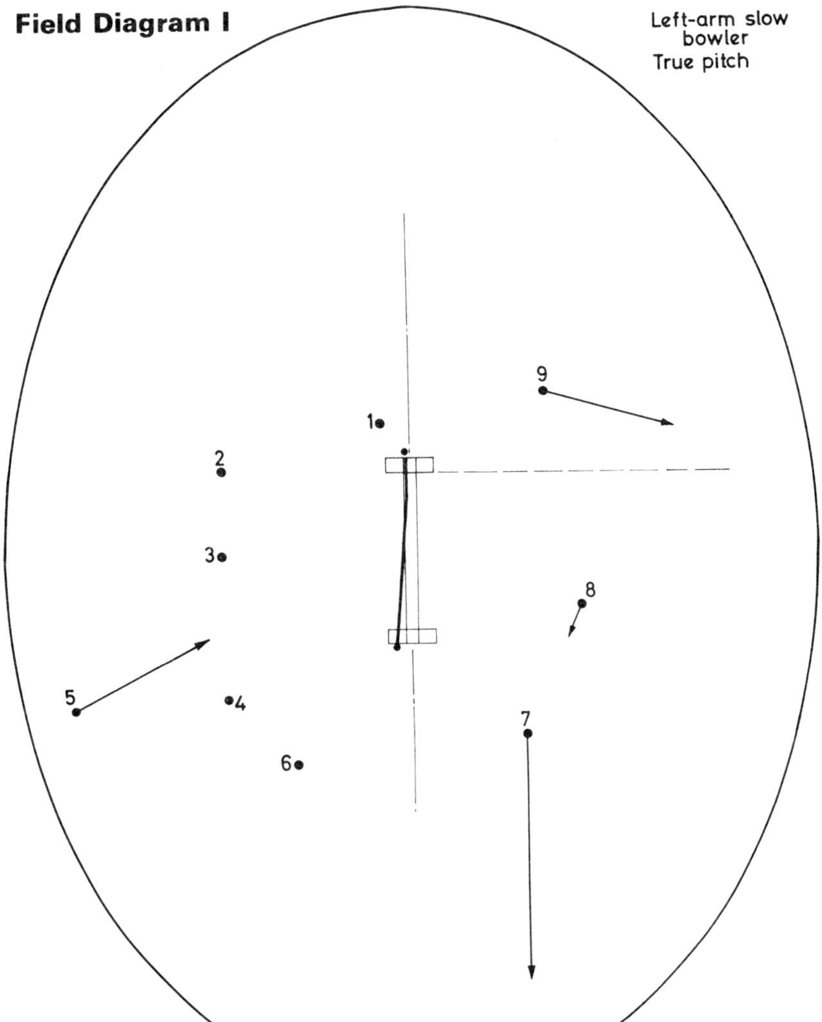

6 on off-side
1 Slip
2 Square-cover-point
3 Cover-point
4 Extra-cover
5 Deep-extra-cover
6 Deep-mid-off

3 on on-side
7 Mid-on
8 Mid-wicket
9 Short-fine-leg

The exact position of the leg-side field will depend on the type of batsman.

Field Diagram J

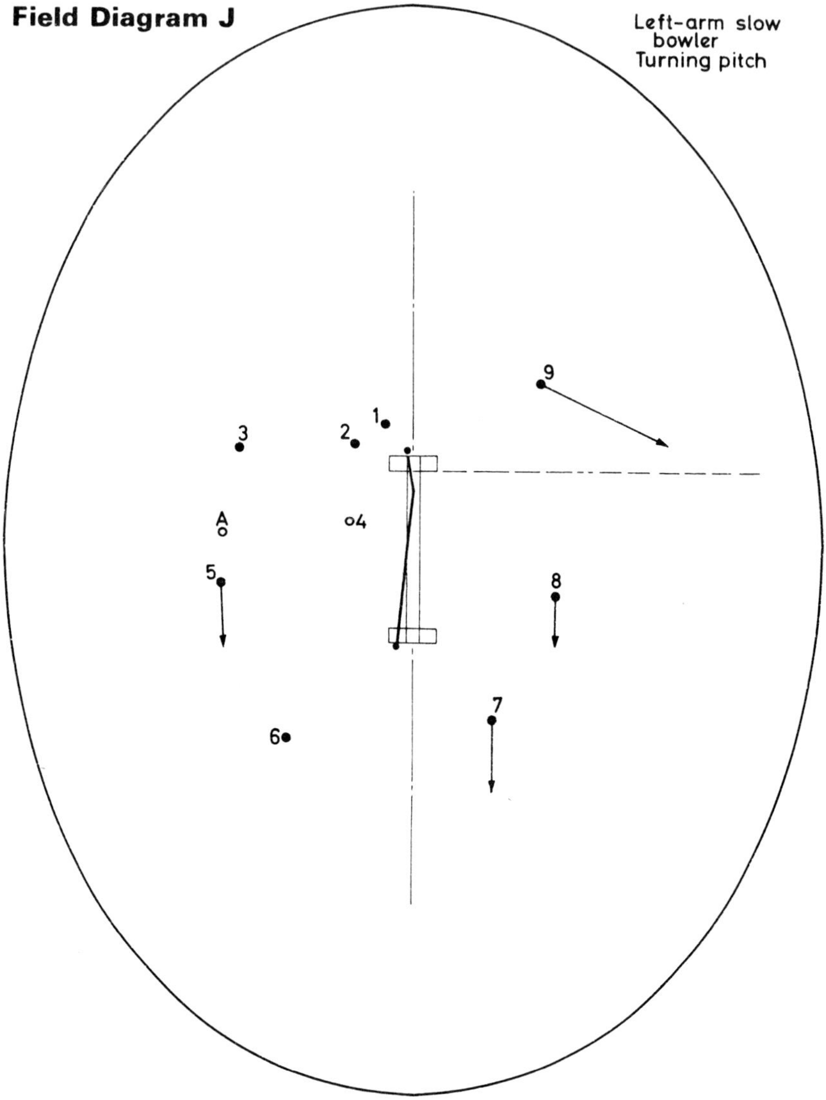

6 on off-side
1 First-slip
2 Second-slip
3 Short-third-man
4 Silly-mid-off
5 Cover
6 Mid-off

3 on on-side
7 Mid-on
8 Mid-wicket
9 Backward-short-leg

Against an attacking batsman an extra fielder will be needed in the covers (A) instead of No. 4. The position of the leg-side field will also depend on the batsman.

Hedley Verity. The great left-arm bowler perfectly positioned for bowling round the wicket *The Photo Source/Central Press*

Derek Underwood. The left-arm bowler follows through after his quicker ball *Patrick Eagar*

batsman, to dispense with one or more of his close fielders. Seldom should he need a deep-square-leg and the more sharply he can turn the ball the wider will his slip and gully be stationed.

The tactics of the left-hander who bowls the wrist-spun 'Chinaman', i.e. the ball turning in to the batsman, will roughly correspond with those of the right-hand off-spinner. A slip is essential for the ball which he must hope the batsman will edge off his googly, or the one which goes straight on. To a left-handed batsman he will aim at the middle and leg stump, with one or two slips, according to how much the ball is turning.

5

Batting

The object of this section of the book is to analyse the principles of technique, which must always be the basis of good batsmanship: but the successful operation of that technique will hinge on other factors.

Of these the most important is that which is commonly termed 'ball sense', which in the case of batting means the ability to sight the ball and judge its length quickly, and then deal with it effectively. Closely allied to this is that indefinable something called 'timing', the ease of physical co-ordination which allows attacking strokes to be played without apparent effort. Ball sense develops from a vast experience of ball play, often from infancy, long before a child has come to the game of cricket. Some, of course, have more natural aptitude than others and acquire 'ball sense' more easily. An experienced coach may sense it, or the lack of it, almost at his first sight of a boy with a bat in his hands. Some do not develop it at all: most of these will probably not want to play cricket, or indeed any other ball game, and it is very doubtful whether they should be made to do so, for to them, such activities may well be a waste of time and a vexation of spirit. **There are others who, though with less natural gift, long to be cricketers: for these, no coaching effort is too great or more rewarding, for the spirit that is in them deserves any success they may be helped to attain.** If, by playing cricket, some contribution is made to a youngster's all-round development, then the exercise has been very well worth the effort.

Of those gifted children no more need be said than that they owe it to themselves and to their coach to make the most of their ability. Nothing is more discouraging than to see real talent wasted by lack of enthusiasm.

But by far the greater majority are those who have some ability and need all the help that can be given to make the best of it: given that help and the willingness to avail themselves of it, most of them can become at the least competent batsmen: it is with these that the coach's main work lies.

The next factor to be considered is not physical at all: it may be bluntly defined as character: it plays a large part in batting and the coach must try to instil it and develop it.

No doubt, what is commonly known as 'match temperament', the instinct to welcome and rise to a big occasion, is in the main part of an individual's psychological 'make-up': but a great deal can be done to build up the right attitude of mind and to acquire self-control: this is an essential reinforcement to technique.

Too much stress cannot be laid on the importance of concentration at the wicket, and the hard work necessary to build up that habit of mind. Batting really consists of playing one ball at a time and the batsman has to learn to concentrate on each ball as it is bowled with maximum vigilance and determination. Once a ball has been bowled, and played, it must be dismissed from the mind, so that full attention can be given to the next one.

A very great batsman used to say that it took him at least a fortnight's regular net practice at the start of the season before he felt he was really looking at the ball. The coach must stress how important it is to work at this habit of concentration by a sustained effort of will in every innings, whether at the nets or in the middle: he will emphasize that one lapse in vigilance, one careless stroke, may cost him his wicket and, perhaps, even victory to his side. Most players at least start their innings with some concentration, but this tends to evaporate as runs come and time passes and they perhaps feel that to some extent they have justified themselves. The coach must persuade a batsman that it is criminal to get out through carelessness or over-confidence later in an innings. If a batsman reaches 50 the applause that greets it should be a signal metaphorically to 'take guard again' and, of course, always with an eye on the clock and score, start to get 50 more.

Every batsman must realize that his duty is first, last, and all the time to his side and not to himself; the more he realizes this the stronger will be his resolve at the start and throughout his innings.

Confidence is a great factor in batting and this, to some extent, is part of a player's natural 'make-up', but it too can be helped by the coach. In a few, especially after a run of success, it may need tempering, though in the long run the game itself will look after that, but with the majority it needs constant building up.

However critical a coach may feel it necessary to be at practice or in a talk after a match, **the overall note of his coaching must be encouragement.** He will be wise to avoid too much technical criticism and concentrate on reinforcing each batsman's belief in himself.

If on the eve of a match his best batsman is conscious of a recent run of failures, the coach must remind him that even the greatest players have often felt the same and have suddenly broken through to play a match-winning innings.

No daunting reputation of the opposition's bowlers must be allowed to make a player forget that batting consists of playing one ball at a time, no matter by whom it is bowled, and that determination, concentration and a sound technique must sooner or later bring their reward in runs.

A good coach will somehow manage to make his batsmen feel that the more formidable the enemy the more inspiring is the challenge, calling for just that extra bit of resolve from everyone in the team which may make the difference between victory and defeat.

Then there is the factor which may be called 'cricket sense', the faculty of deciding rightly what tactics to pursue in any given situation and against any given bowler, when to take a risk and when to concentrate on defence, of judging how best to counter a particular field setting or some special difficulty of the pitch. This must, of course, come mainly by experience but the coach can help his players to acquire it by explaining the lessons to be learnt from each day's play and encouraging an intelligent approach. He must try to make them understand that **even the champions are always learning.**

An offensive spirit is essential and must be harnessed to technique. To win matches a batsman must make runs: though a sound defence is necessary to stay long at the crease his purpose must be, wherever and as soon as possible, to wrest the initiative from the bowler and to retain it.

Obviously, some players are by temperament more disposed to attack than others, but the **coach must aim at developing some attacking strokes** in all his players and above all instilling in them the will to attack.

The greatest problem in the teaching of batting is how to impart the artificial technique of straight-bat play and at the same time fostering the natural instinct to hit the ball and enjoy hitting it.

To cramp players with purely defensive technique, still more to curb their offensive spirit, is the worst of coaching sins.

In cricket, as in other games, genius may often seem to defy the normally accepted rules, although this defiance may often be more apparent than real. Unorthodoxy can be a valuable asset: however, all players must have, and be able to return to, a basic technique as and when the situation dictates.

It is now getting on for 200 years since the bowler began to try to 'pitch a length' and the batsman discovered the only logical answer to it and the **first principle of his art was that the longer the face of the bat on the line of the ball, the better chance he had of meeting it.** No matter what changes there have been in stroke play since then, and may be in the future, it must be true that the straight bat, moving down the line of the ball, is the basis of good batting.

By far the most important, and most difficult, task of any coach in batting is to train the young batsman to play straight: to this end, he should train him to strengthen his top hand, for it is the top hand that guides in every straight-bat stroke, and at the same time keeps the bottom hand under control. Unfortunately, this is not the most natural method of hitting a ball, for it is the bottom hand which usually tends to dominate.

N.B. Everything that follows is written for a right-hand batsman: for a left-hander reverse 'left' and 'right'.

GRIP

A correct grip is of great importance if the hands are to work together and so ensure control and power in playing strokes on both sides of the wicket.

The batsman should find that:

1. **The hands are close together with the left hand near the top of the handle.**
2. **If the bat is upright and the face is to the bowler, the back of the left hand aims somewhere between mid-off and extra-cover.**
3. **The fingers and thumbs of both hands are well round the handle, the left hand gripping firmly.**
4. **The V formed by the first finger and thumb of the left hand is directly over the corresponding V of the right and the line of these V's is between the outer edge of the bat and the splice** (Figs. 1 and 2).

Fig. 1.
Grip:
hands close together:
Vs of the hands on same line, between outside edge and splice

TAKING GUARD

The object in taking guard is to enable the batsman to know exactly where he is in relation to the stumps and to be in the best position to sight the

Fig. 2.
Grip: as seen by the bowler: left hand is resting comfortably against inside of left thigh; back of left hand, so positioned, faces bowler

ball. His guard should therefore be such that his head is in line with the middle stump and his eyes level. A batsman with a naturally upright stance may prefer a guard on centre, or middle and leg stumps: if he is inclined to stoop he will be safer with leg stump. In asking for a guard he should hold the bat upright with its face to the umpire who can then see clearly which stump or stumps it will be covering. It is quite unnecessary to dig a pit with the bat after taking guard. All the batsman needs to do is make a mark to show him where he stands relative to the stumps. He will expect, and if necessary ask, the umpire to give him guard from directly behind and over the bowler's wicket: that is the line by which the umpire will adjudge an l.b.w. decision.

STANCE

An easy and balanced stance is important, for the back-lift and all strokes spring from it. It conditions the proper watching of the ball and the proper moving of the feet.

Figs. 3 & 4.
The stance:
feet comfortably apart and parallel with crease: left shoulder pointing down the pitch and eyes level

Stances in fact vary widely in detail and no batsman should be forced to stand in a way which he finds uncomfortable. But most good batsmen conform to the following principles:

The feet

1. The heels should be equally spaced just either side of the popping crease. The right foot should be parallel with, or pointing just behind, the crease and the left foot roughly parallel with it, though many batsmen find it more natural to point it more towards cover and indeed deliberately open their stance when facing in-swing or off-spin bowling. The toes of both feet should be just clear of the line of the leg stump.
2. **The weight should be equally balanced between the feet and never on the heels.**
3. The knees should be very slightly relaxed, making for easy and quick movement.
4. **There should be no movement of the feet until the length of the ball is judged and the actual stroke begins.**

The body

The body should be sideways, facing cover-point: the more directly the left shoulder can point at the opposite wicket, the easier will be the correct and straight back-lift, but this must on no account be exaggerated or the stance will become artificial and strained.

The head

The head must be kept upright and turned towards the bowler with the eyes as level as possible; only so can the batsman focus both eyes together and command a proper sight and judgement of the ball; **the head must be kept as still as possible.**

The expression 'two-eyed stance' is frequently used when it is in fact a 'two-shouldered stance': this is when feet and shoulders open up to the bowler, thus making for a faulty back-lift and cross-bat play.

The bat

Most players find it natural and comfortable to ground the bat just behind the toes of the right foot and just to the off side of them, with the blade facing in slightly to the left leg and the hands at ease just touching the left thigh. But here again the batsman should feel comfortable and 'at the ready' (Figs. 3 and 4).

The more upright a batsman can stand, the more likely he is to be well

Peter May. The stance: the shoulder pointing at the bowler, the head fully turned, and the eyes level
J. G. Dunbar

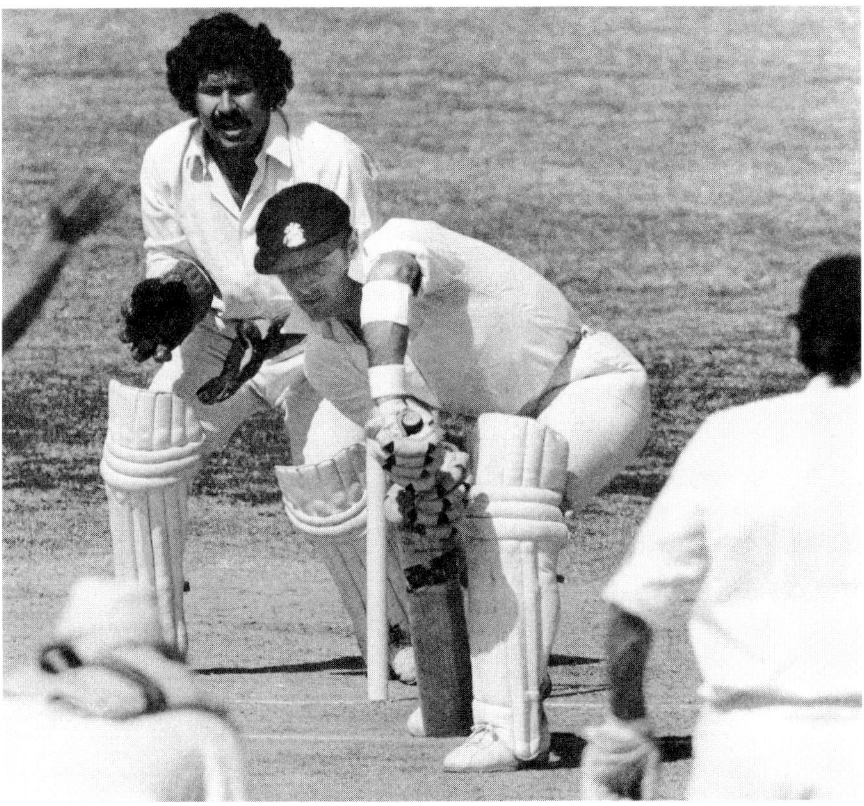

Geoffrey Boycott. The forward defensive stroke: the left foot has moved well out and the left knee is slightly bent to 'shut the gate'. The high front elbow and relaxed grip of the right hand ensures ball is played down
Patrick Eagar

W. G. Grace. 'The doctor' knew it all years ago! The right foot has moved well back, the position of the head and shoulder is perfect, the face of the bat is fully open, and the top hand is firmly in control

Jack Hobbs. 'The master' plays the pull: the balance and position of the feet are perfect *Press Association*

Ian Botham. The left shoulder and head are leading into the line of an off-drive: good back lift and foot well to the pitch of the ball
Patrick Eagar

Viv Richards. Perfect finish of a powerful off-drive
Patrick Eagar

balanced and to have his eyes level. Occasionally, a very tall batsman may find it easier to get his eyes level if his bat does not touch the ground at all.

THE BACK-LIFT

A correct back-lift is not 'natural' and too much attention cannot be paid to getting it right. Although it is true that some gifted batsmen lift the bat wide of the slips they so adjust it that in all straight-bat strokes the bat starts its downward movement at the top of the line of the intended stroke. For straight balls the movement will begin from a point directly above the wicket; the wider the ball is to the off and the wider the stroke is aimed, the more must the initial turn of the left shoulder start the downward movement of the bat from the direction of fine-leg; for balls on, or just outside the leg stump, the slight dipping and opening of the left shoulder will start the downward movement of the bat from the line of slip.

The principle must hold true that the straighter the back-lift, the better must be the prospect of the whole stroke being played straight. The bat should be picked up with both hands but with the left, i.e. top, hand dominating, the left arm being pushed back far enough to give a slight feeling of tension in the left shoulder; the left elbow will bend slightly and the wrist will cock, thus naturally opening the face of the bat. **At the top of the back-lift the left wrist will be at least level with, and preferably above, the left elbow: the right elbow will also have bent and the right wrist will also be higher than the elbow** (Fig. 5).

The control of the left hand is essential. If the right hand grips too tightly and takes charge it may tend to take the bat towards third-man. If both hands are pushed slightly back, it will help to ensure that the left shoulder is kept pointing down the pitch.

Nearly all great batsmen pick their hands well up, and though it is true that they commit themselves later to the stroke and yet have time in which to play it, the average player will find that the late back-lift will almost certainly produce a hurried and crooked stroke. Against fast bowling the back-lift should be earlier: young players will do well to pick up the bat as the bowler is releasing the ball.

Common faults

Grip 1. Having the hands too far apart with the right hand too low on the handle: this prevents the hands from working in unison as is necessary in all straight-bat strokes, and encourages the right hand to take charge and to warp the line of the stroke.

Fig. 5.
The back-lift:
the left arm has pushed the bat back over the stumps: the hands are high: the face of the bat is open: the eyes are looking squarely at the ball

2. Having the back of the left hand behind the handle, thus restricting the stroke.

Both of these faults may be caused by the bat being too big or too heavy.

Stance

1. Feet too far apart: this prejudices initial movement.
2. Stance too 'open': this encourages a crooked back-lift and makes it difficult to lead with the head and left shoulder into straight-bat strokes on the off-side.
3. Head not turned to face down the wicket, and eyes not as level as possible.
4. Head not in line with the stumps.
5. Head taken too far over to the off-side, causing a loss of balance.

Back-lift

1. Right hand too much in control.
2. Right elbow higher than wrist so that the face of the bat cannot open.
3. Picking the bat up too late.

THE FORWARD AND BACK STROKES

These two strokes constitute the basis of all good batting, whether in attack or defence; indeed all cricket strokes are really adaptations of one or the other.

Correct footwork is an essential part of all stroke play. It is often said of a great batsman that he is great because he moves his feet well: this implies that, because he possesses perfect judgement, he is able to position his feet correctly and at the right moment, without ever being hurried or off balance.

The greatest advance in batting technique which has taken place since the turn of the century has been the development of back play. Whereas previously, most batsmen would push forward to meet the ball of awkward length, the majority of top class batsmen today would tend to play it off the back foot, thereby enabling themselves to watch it off the pitch: the more difficult the wicket and the more the ball is turning, the more they rely on back play unless, of course, they are able to smother it by playing right forward with a dead bat. This radical change in technique has undoubtedly led to a great strengthening in defence.

In the last two decades, however, a tendency has developed, particularly among the less gifted batsmen, to return to the front foot in defence. This has probably come about as a result of the change in the l.b.w. law, introduced in 1935, and the gradual appreciation on the part of the batsman that it is more difficult for an umpire to give an l.b.w. decision on the front foot. It is significant that this practice is more prevalent in this country than elsewhere because the conditions are more favourable to the bowlers.

Whilst the saying 'When in doubt, push out' may in certain circumstances be a safety measure, if carried to the extreme it must inevitably reduce the batsman's range of strokes. Equally concentration on back foot play will impose its limitations. Either will make the bowler's task less difficult.

But when all is said and done, it is beyond doubt that **almost all great batsmen have been ready and able to play off either foot, according to the length of the ball, with equal facility.**

It must be the aim of every coach to develop this facility in all who are placed in his charge. He must never allow a young cricketer to think of defence in terms of back play and attack in terms of forward: both strokes can be played either defensively or offensively.

In the following sections these strokes will first be analysed as played defensively, only because their basic principles can thus be more easily understood and practised. But when teaching them, the coach must drive it home that they do not just offer a means of survival but also the mechanism for attack which every batsman must acquire as soon as possible.

THE FORWARD STROKE

The forward stroke varies little whether played straight, to the off or to the on: the main difference is the direction in which the head and left shoulder move out on to the line of the ball and the position of the left foot. As previously mentioned, the mechanism of the stroke is basically the same whether played in defence or in attack (the Drives).

The head

In all forward strokes the left shoulder with the head close to it, must lead out and on to the line of the ball. If a batsman can be taught to think of this, he will find that his left foot and the balance of his body must automatically follow.

The eyes must watch – really watch – the ball as nearly on to the bat as possible.

The left shoulder and left hip

The position of the left shoulder and left hip is fundamental to all forward strokes. The line of the shoulders initially should be parallel to that of the intended stroke.

The wider the stroke is aimed to the off, the more should the back of the shoulder be turned on the bowler.

For strokes aimed at or wide of mid-on, the shoulder and hip should lead in that direction but must never be allowed to fall away from the stroke, for this will at once pull the bat across the line of the ball.

The left foot

The left foot will move out as far as possible towards the pitch of the ball and as near as possible to its line. The nearer it can get to the pitch the less room there is for the ball to alter direction after pitching: the nearer it can get to the line, the less gap there will be between bat and pad.

The left knee must bend slightly to allow the weight of the body to come through on to the front foot and into the stroke thus helping to 'shut the gate' between bat and front leg. The head should be just in front of the left foot and in line with the ball.

For straight balls the toe of the left foot will point approximately towards extra-cover. The wider the ball is to the off, the wider will the left toe point. For balls on the leg stump the left foot will be found to have moved slightly to the on-side as a consequence of the head and shoulder leading on to the line of the ball.

Fig. 6.
The forward stroke in defence: head and eyes on the line of the ball: left shoulder, arm, and hand in control, presenting full face of the bat: left knee slightly bent to 'shut the gate'

Fig. 7. The forward stroke in defence: the batsman has made full use of his reach: bat meets ball just in front of the left foot and virtually below the eyes

The right foot

The heel of the right foot will naturally ease to allow the weight of the body to come forward on to the left foot: at the end of the stroke only the inside of the toe of the right foot will be on the ground. If the right foot is allowed to pivot the left hip and shoulder may turn and cause the batsman to play across the line of the ball.

The hands

The left hand must control the whole shape of the stroke. At the moment of impact the left hand will be slightly in advance of the right: this ensures the ball being kept down (Fig. 6).

Some experienced players may occasionally turn this hand towards the back of the handle when seeking additional reach to smother the ball. But young batsmen must beware of making a habit of this as in no other stroke must the firm grip of the left hand or its position be varied.

The right hand will, as the bat comes forward, relax its grip into one between the thumb and the first two fingers. **It is impossible to play any defensive forward stroke correctly if the bat continues to be gripped in the palm of the right hand.**

The bat

The longer the full face of the bat is on the path of the ball, the more secure must be the stroke. When the stroke is played defensively, i.e. to balls of good length, the bat will meet the ball as near its pitch as possible without the batsman overstretching; against off-spinners and in-swingers, the bat will meet the ball level with the pad. **There will be no follow-through; the full face of the bat will remain held on the line of the ball with the handle of the bat ahead of the blade** (Fig. 7).

Common faults

1. Not leading with the head and left shoulder out on to the line of the ball.
2. Not taking the left foot far enough forward, and not bending the left knee.
3. Not keeping the inside of the right foot on the ground.
4. Not making the left hand and arm control the stroke.
5. Not moving the full face of the bat along the line of the ball.

THE DRIVES

The player who cannot drive is only half a batsman. Not only does he lack the most exhilarating and productive weapon of attack, but, in lacking it,

Fig. 8.
The start of the off-drive: the left shoulder has turned to lead on to the intended line of the stroke: the left hip has not been allowed to fall away: the head, close to the left shoulder, is looking down the line of the ball

Fig. 9.
The finish of an off-drive: the head, body and the straight left arm have led right through on the line of the stroke: the wrists will 'break' later

he greatly simplifies the bowler's task and enables him to win and to hold the initiative by keeping the ball well up. Conversely, a batsman who can drive, especially if he can use his feet, can wrest the initiative from the bowler, and, by inducing him to bowl short, greatly simplify his own defence, especially on slow and turning pitches. This is also inevitably reflected in the placing of the field; if, by his ability and readiness to drive, the batsman can force the bowler to place one or more men in defensive positions he makes it impossible for him to maintain a network of close-set attacking fielders.

The general mechanism of the drive is the same as that of the forward stroke in defence, but operating on an extended and accelerated arc. The head and left shoulder will still lead: for the off-drive the initial movement of 'turning the back to the bowler' is most noticeable in all the great exponents of this stroke (Fig. 8). The left hip will be kept close to the intended line of the stroke and the left arm will control the arc. But the arc of the drive will begin with a freer and higher back-lift and will be kept as long and flat as possible with both arms following right through the line of the stroke until the natural break of the wrists takes place.

The longer the blade of the bat is kept on the path of the ball the better, and this is facilitated if the left arm is kept as close to the body as possible in the back swing and the right arm as close as possible as the bat comes through. In the timed acceleration of the arc the right hand powerfully reinforces the left, but on no account must it be allowed to become the dominant hand, or to shut the face of the bat before impact.

For drives along the ground the ball will be met at a point just beyond the left toe, but all really good drivers have been able and ready to drive the ball in the air over the head of the bowler, mid-off and mid-on: for this lofted drive the ball must be met a little earlier, i.e. at a point further in front of the left foot and there must be a full follow-through of the bat.

When the ball is slow and its trajectory high enough to give the batsman time, he can drive 'quick-footed', moving down the pitch in a smooth *chassé*. After the initial step with the left foot, the right foot will work up behind it thus keeping the left shoulder up to the ball and preventing the weight from falling away from the stroke; this movement must be kept as smooth as possible in order that the head may remain level and so continue to focus the ball accurately (Figs. 12 and 13).

At the end of a well-hit drive, the batsman should find himself with his weight firmly balanced on his front foot, with his head still leading, and knowing that the whole face of the bat was moving down the line of the ball at the moment of impact.

Power in driving comes from the long swing of the arms, the timed transference of weight, and wrist work just before contact with the ball. Again the batsmen must be warned against 'pressing': this generally takes the form of the right hand and right shoulder coming in too early causing

Tom Graveney. A great front foot player: perfectly balanced; his head has led; arms and hands have gone up the line *The Photo Source/Sport & General*

David Gower. The same stroke, only played squarer by the elegant left-hander *Patrick Eagar*

Barry Richards. Hitting straight over the bowler's head: the perfect finish
Patrick Eagar

Don Bradman. The great batsman demonstrates foot work at its very best during his famous 254 v England at Lord's in 1930

Geoffrey Boycott. A perfect on-drive by a great technician *Patrick Eagar*

Mike Gatting. The modern square drive: a valuable run scoring stroke, provided the head and front foot are well to the pitch of the ball *Patrick Eagar*

Fig. 10.
The start of an on-drive: the left shoulder has dipped slightly and the left foot has opened to lead the body on to the line of the stroke

Fig. 11.
The finish of an on-drive: the head has led the full transference of weight on to the front foot

the head and body to rise and preventing the blade of the bat being kept on the line of the ball.

In teaching the off-drive the coach will do well to stress the supreme importance of the head and left shoulder: the wider the ball the more should the batsman turn his back to the bowler and the more, in fact, will the bat start its downward movement from the direction of fine-leg. Young batsmen should be warned that the 'quick-footed' drive to the wide off ball is a difficult stroke, involving as it does a movement not only down the pitch but outwards as well.

Most coaches will agree that young players find no stroke more difficult to master than the on-drive. Their great difficulty seems to lie in the transference of the line of balance to the on-side and the relative opening up of the left foot on which this depends. They will find that if they will slightly drop the left shoulder, keeping the side of the face close to it, this will naturally lead the left foot to move out on the right line (Figs. 10 and 11).

Very few boys under the age of 14 or so have the strength necessary to drive with any effect and security but, as soon as they have, the coach should regard it as one of his chief duties to initiate and encourage them in this, the most satisfying of all cricket strokes.

Common faults

1. Not picking the hands and bat well up.
2. Not leading with the head and left shoulder so as to bring the eyes and body balance on to the line of the ball.
3. Not getting the left foot out and close enough to the pitch of the ball.
4. Allowing the right hand to come into the stroke too early so that the arc is shortened and pulled across the line instead of being kept long, flat and smooth, with the bat face travelling down the line for as long as possible.
5. Trying to hit too hard with consequent loss of balance.
6. Allowing the right foot to pivot.

THE BACK-STROKE IN DEFENCE

All great players have the ability to play off the back foot equally as well as off the front.

The hallmark of good back play is the use the batsman makes of the ground between the creases: the further he moves his right foot back, the longer he has to watch the ball and the easier it is to play it: he can thus, in fact, turn the length ball into one comfortably short of a length, and the

Figs. 12 & 13.
Moving out to drive: following the first stride, the right foot has moved up just behind the left foot, thus enabling the left shoulder to keep leading down the line

ball just short of a length into one that can be dealt with by an attacking stroke.

The second principle is that the right foot should move not only back but as far on to the line of the ball as possible, so that the bat, swinging down straight from a high back-lift, has just room to clear the right pad as it moves down the line.

Thirdly, the back-stroke, like the forward stroke, must be played from a sideways position and is controlled with the left arm and wrist; only so can the face of the bat be kept moving down the line of the ball.

The mechanism of the stroke can now be analysed:

The feet

The initial movement of the back foot is of the utmost importance – well back and on to the line of the ball. **To ensure that it lands parallel to the crease the shoulder will be kept pointing towards the bowler.** The foot will land firmly and flat; in the case of the straight ball it will be more or less parallel to the crease: if the ball is outside the off stump and the stroke is to be aimed at mid-off or wider, the toes will point just backwards of the crease: for the ball pitching on or just outside the leg stump, the foot will again be parallel but the hips will open up to mid-on (Fig. 14).

The left foot follows the right, finishing in a position of natural balance close to it, with the heel released and the toe some inches in front of the right foot's instep and pointing to extra-cover.

The body and head

Though inevitably following the right foot as it moves back, it is important that the body and the head should keep their forward poise. At the moment of impact the line of balance on the braced right leg will be forward and into the stroke, the head kept down immediately above the bat handle and directly behind the line of the ball.

The arms and hands

The left arm and wrist lead and control the stroke. **From a high back-lift the left elbow will be high at the moment of impact:** the right hand will open into a finger and thumb grip (Figs. 14 and 15).

The bat

The full face of the bat will move down the line of the ball with the hands slightly in advance of the blade at the moment of impact. In the defensive back-stroke there will be no follow-through.

Fig. 14. The start of a back-stroke: the right foot has moved well back, parallel with the crease: the left shoulder, arm and hand are in full control

Fig. 15. The back-stroke: note the high left elbow, the relaxed grip of the right hand and the left heel just eased

Common faults

1. Not stepping far enough back with the right foot and not moving far enough over to get on to the line of the delivery.
2. Not picking the hands up high enough in the back-lift to allow the ball to be played down.
3. Not keeping sideways to the line of the stroke.
4. Not keeping the head and balance of the body forward when making contact with the ball.
5. Not making the left hand control the bat and keeping its face on the line of the ball and not allowing the right hand to relax into a thumb and finger grip.
6. Not keeping the left elbow up high enough.

THE BACK-STROKE IN ATTACK

The safest of all methods of forcing for runs a ball that is short of a length is by an attacking back-stroke played past the braced right leg.

To play this stroke effectively, the batsman must make the most of his height, even rising slightly on the toes of his right foot. He will also have to give himself a little more 'room' than in the case of the defensive back-stroke.

The bat swing, as with the drive, will be lengthened and accelerated: the left arm will still control the arc of the stroke, but the right hand, still with a thumb and finger grip, will reinforce it with a punch just before impact.

In playing the stroke the elbows will be slightly bent: **the body must be kept sideways, with great emphasis on the head being kept down and forward:** the wider the ball is on the off, the more must the back of the left shoulder be turned on the bowler.

The face of the bat will be kept full on the line of the stroke for as long as possible, and on no account must the head and the line of balance be allowed to fall away (Fig. 16).

The power comes from the acceleration of the hands and the uncocking of the wrists just before impact with the ball. Batsmen must be warned against 'pressing', i.e. trying to hit too hard: this invariably leads to loss of balance and rhythm and with them much of the power, or results in a mis-hit.

STROKES PLAYED WITH A HORIZONTAL BAT

Though the straight bat moving down the line of the ball is the basis of batting security, some of the most effective scoring strokes are those played

Fig. 16.
The forcing back-stroke: the left arm is in control; the full face of the bat has been kept open on the line of the stroke

with a relatively 'cross', i.e. horizontal, bat. Moreover these strokes, in which the bottom hand dominates, are by far the more natural.

Most of all is this true of the full-pitch or the long-hop on or outside the line of the stumps and **it has been well said that in most junior cricket the side that never bowled to leg and that hit every leg-side delivery would never lose a match.** Yet how often, in fact, are they missed, unless the stroke is played correctly, and above all, unless the batsman gets and keeps his head on the line and really watches the ball.

The coach can offer young cricketers no earlier or more certain dividend in runs than by combining with the technique of straight-bat defence the method by which they can effectively and consistently deal with the full-pitch or long-hop. This may be analysed as follows:

Fig. 17. Hitting a full-pitch to leg: the head and left leg have led out on to the line: the ball will be hit at full stretch of the arms at, or in front of, square-leg

HITTING A FULL-PITCH TO LEG

The head

As with all strokes the position of the head is of paramount importance: in hitting the full-pitch the head leads the body which will move forward and over on to the line of the ball. Once there, with eyes looking straight down the line of flight, it must be kept still and on no account be allowed to sway over to the on-side with the impetus of the stroke.

The feet

The left foot will move forward and, if the ball is wide of the leg stump, outward on to its line: it will land pointing more or less down the pitch.

The body

The body will follow the lead of the head so that at the moment of impact with the ball its weight will be full on the left leg which has been allowed to bend allowing the body to come through into the stroke.

The bat

It is most important to get the bat out and on to the line of the ball early so

Greg Chappell plays a forcing back-stroke through the covers: his weight is on the back foot, which is parallel to the crease;, and the poise of the body is forwards *All-Sport/Adrian Murrell*

Ted Dexter v Wes Hall. A magnificent example of getting behind the line of a fast, rising ball

Martin Crowe. Perfect balance for a powerful 'blow' off the back foot *All-Sport/Adrian Murrell*

Denis Compton. The finish of a hook outside the leg stump: the right hand has rolled over the left

Mike Gatting. The finish of the pull stroke: the left leg has been taken well across, and the head is in the line of the ball *All-Sport/Michael King*

that it can be struck with the arms at full stretch in front of the left leg: it cannot be properly hit if the elbows are tucked in (Fig. 17). The bat should hit the ball with the full face: the straighter the delivery, the more in front of square-leg should the stroke be aimed.

N.B. A full-pitch in line with the stumps and below knee height at the moment of impact should be driven with a straight bat.

The main reasons why the full-pitch is so frequently missed or ineffectively hit are:

1. Not getting the head on to the line of the ball and not looking at it; not making sure that at the completion of the stroke the head is still facing straight down the pitch.
2. Not freeing the elbows from the body so that the bat can strike the ball with arms almost at full stretch.
3. Hitting late and aiming the stroke too fine.
4. Hitting too hard thus swaying the body off balance causing the head to move and the sighting of the ball to be impaired.

THE PULL

The pull and the hook (described later) are similar in that they are both cross-bat strokes in which a ball, even on or just outside the off stump, is hit on to the on side. The difference lies in the fact that the pull is played to a ball regardless of its pace whereas the hook is played to a fast short-pitched ball which has bounced at least chest high.

The feet

As in all back play, **the first and vital move in the execution of this stroke is to take the right foot back well towards the stumps: the further and earlier it moves, the longer will the batsman have to watch the ball and the greater will be his command of it.**

But whereas in the other back-strokes the right foot will land facing cover-point and just sufficiently inside the line of the ball to allow the bat face to move down it, it will now, in hitting the long-hop, move just to off of that line and the foot will land pointing to extra-cover or even straighter. The left leg will be taken to the leg side to a point level with, or even a little in front of, the right thus opening up the body square to the line of flight. The wider the ball is to leg, the further will the left foot be carried away to the on-side, i.e. the wider the gap between the right and left feet when set for the stroke; the object being in every case to get the head on to the line of the ball. Both knees will be slightly flexed, to ensure that the weight is kept forward.

Fig. 18.
The start of the pull:
the right foot has moved well back and opened, and the left foot back and across to bring the head on to the line: the balance is still forward and the ball is met at full stretch of the arms

Fig. 19.
The finish of the pull:
the right hand has climbed over the left to keep the ball down:
the weight is on the left leg: the head is still facing down the pitch

Fig. 20.
The start of the hook:
The right foot has gone well back and across, the head is just to the off-side of the line of the ball, and there is a high back lift of bat

Fig. 21.
The finish of a hook:
the body has pivoted and the right hand climbed over the left to keep the ball down

The head

The head and body are placed directly in line with the ball. The forward poise of the body is most important: the head must be kept very still with the eyes 'glued' on the ball. At the completion of the stroke the weight of the body will be fully on the left leg (Fig. 18).

The bat

Both hands will maintain their full grip on the handle. Commencing with a high back-lift the bat will follow the body turn. From there, a combination of wrists and arms will fling the bat down and across the body, to meet the ball at full arm's stretch.

In this movement the right hand will dominate and the right wrist will tend to shut the face of the bat: this, plus the transference of the weight to the left leg, will ensure the ball is hit down: the more the direction of the stroke is aimed towards mid-wicket the less chance there is of the batsman being late on the ball (Fig. 19).

The reasons why the long-hop is frequently missed or badly struck are similar to those for the full-pitch (*see* page 95) with one addition: the body not being in the right position, i.e. completely open-chested to the bowler.

THE HOOK

As already mentioned, the hook is played to a fast short-pitched ball which has bounced at least chest high.

To play it with safety, **it is essential that the batsman moves his weight early and well on to his right foot, which has not only moved back but also far enough across to be just on the off-side of the line of flight.** He will thus by quick footwork give himself as much time as possible to watch the ball off the pitch and ensure that, if he misses it, it will pass over or by his left shoulder.

The mechanics of the stroke are similar to those described for the pull shot except that the body is on the off-side of the line of the ball: this will result in the ball being struck behind square-leg.

This stroke, though very profitable when played correctly, is only mastered with experience: it should not be attempted until the batsman has had time to gauge the pace and bounce of the pitch (Figs. 20 and 21).

THE SWEEP

A slow ball of good length outside the leg stump can only be driven with safety if the batsman has time to move down the pitch to make it into a half-volley. To such a ball the sweep is a valuable alternative, in that it is an attacking stroke, the ball being hit into the part of the field where at most there can be no more than two fieldsmen.

The head

The head will lead the body out on to the line of the ball.

The feet

The left foot will follow the initial movement of the head and will land directly in line with the delivery. On landing the left leg will start to bend bringing the trunk into a slightly forward position: the right leg will also be flexed.

The bat

As in hitting the full-toss to leg, it is important to get the bat out on to the line of the ball early so that it can be struck with the arms at full stretch in front of the bent front leg.

At the point of contact the bat will be almost horizontal. To ensure the ball is struck down the bat is kept just on top of the line of flight and the wrists are allowed to close the face slightly.

Dangers in sweeping are:

1. However correctly the stroke is played, if the ball bounces higher than expected, it may go off the top edge.
2. Against a leg-break, if the legs are not positioned correctly, the ball may spin round behind them, possibly out of the bowler's footmark, and hit the stumps.
3. Against an accurate off-spin bowler, is selecting a ball which is not going to miss the wicket: his 'floater', i.e. the ball which goes with his arm *and* holds its line, claims many victims amongst over-keen 'sweepers'.

THE CUT

It is important to remember that the cut must only be employed against the short delivery wide of the off stump. If the ball is pitched short and close to the stumps a forcing stroke off the back foot would be played more safely.

Because the square cut and late cut are played with a cross-bat the margin of error is small, and to cut well and safely demands judgement of length, nicety of timing and flexibility of wrist. Most young batsmen of any ability can find them a valuable method of attack, provided they are helped to master the basic techniques, and can learn to pick the right ball at which to play them: watching the ball in the air and off the pitch is also essential.

It is vital that the batsman should throw his arms and hands outwards and downwards on to the ball. It is difficult to cut balls that are rising high or are pitched close to the stumps: it is particularly dangerous to attempt the stroke to off-spin or in-swing bowling unless the ball is well wide.

The majority of youngsters who have some natural ability will find themselves wanting to cut: the coach must attempt to help them to succeed, insisting above all on the importance of coming down on to the ball from a high back-lift.

The stroke may be played early or late, with the ball struck relatively square or fine of the wicket: in each case the mechanism is basically the same.

The back-lift

The successful execution of the stroke stems largely from a proper back-lift. As the line and length of the ball is sighted and the judgement of the cut made, **the shoulders start to turn and the forearms and wrists moving round the body will not only extend the normal back-lift but take it backwards to square leg or mid wicket.**

The feet

The movement of the right foot will depend on the direction of the stroke: the finer the line of the stroke the further back will the right foot be taken. The right toe will point down that line and the left heel will be freed to allow full weight transference on to the right foot (Fig. 23).

The bat

From the high back-lift the arms and wrists will fling the bat outwards and downwards so that at the moment of impact the wrists will be approximately above the right foot and the bat appreciably behind it.

As contact with the ball is frequently made near the peak of its bounce **it is especially important that the bat comes down on to it from above.** If the right wrist is allowed to roll over it will further help to eliminate the chance of the ball being hit in the air (Fig. 22).

Common faults

1. Not getting the bat up high enough to ensure it comes down on to the ball from above.
2. Cutting too hard instead of using the pace of the ball to help it on its

Fig. 22.
A square-cut: the arms and hands have been 'thrown' out and down into the stroke with the head leading the weight over a bent right knee

Fig. 23.
The finish of a late-cut: The right toe points in the direction of the intended stroke and the batsman's back is almost turned on the bowler: the point of impact is almost level with the stumps

way: this generally results in the batsman either not watching the ball on to the bat or dipping his right shoulder and so tending to get under the ball.

3. Meeting the ball too early: the best cutters strike the ball level with the popping crease: for the late cut they let the ball get almost in line with the stumps before making contact.

THE LEG GLANCE

The beauty and delicacy of this stroke may be regarded as a refinement of batting, the ability to play it being a real asset, provided the batsman recognizes that it is in no sense a substitute for, but only a variation of, the on-side strokes played with the full face of the bat. There is nothing to be said for glancing a ball to fine-leg for one or two when it could have been hit safely wide of mid-on for four.

The chief value of the leg glance is to be found on a fast pitch and against bowlers of some pace, especially when the ball is moving in to the batsman. But with a leg-slip which some bowlers often position to counteract it, it is a dangerous stroke unless the batsman can play the ball down.

The leg glance is really a refinement of the forward and backward defensive strokes, and can be played according to the length of the ball, off either foot. In each case it is played with a straight bat with the face being allowed to shut fractionally as contact is made. **There is therefore very little margin of error and the stroke should never be played to a straight ball. Care must also be taken to ensure that the ball is not played so fine that a catch is given to the wicket-keeper.**

The leg glance off the front foot

The most suitable delivery for this stroke is one that is of good length on or just outside the batsman's pads. As with the forward stroke played towards mid-on, the head and left shoulder will lead the body out and over on to the line of the ball with the front foot landing just inside the line of the ball, so that if it were missed it would hit the outside of the left pad. If the batsman is to have full control of the ball and be able to keep it down, it is most important that he should meet it in front of the left leg and almost directly under the head (Fig. 24).

The leg glance off the back foot

This stroke is played most effectively to the ball pitched just short of a length on, or just outside, the batsman's left leg. Balls that are short should not be glanced but forced in front of the wicket with the full face

Clive Lloyd. The finish of the hook: the body has pivoted and cleared the line of the ball, which has been hit down *Patrick Eagar*

David Gower. Finish of a square cut: the full weight has gone into the stroke and the ball has been kept down *Patrick Eagar*

Fig. 24.
The leg glance off the front foot: the ball has been met just in front of the left leg, with the batsman's head right on the line

Fig. 25.
The leg glance off the back foot: the batsman has moved well back and is deflecting the ball just in front of his left leg: again the head is on the line

of the bat, or if very short, either pulled or hooked, depending on the degree of bounce.

As in the normal back defensive stroke the right leg will be taken well back towards the stumps in order to give the batsman the maximum time in which to watch the ball off the pitch: it must move sufficiently across the wicket to allow the left foot, which follows it, to position itself just inside the line of delivery. The right foot will land with the toes pointing to extra-cover, the left approximately straight down the pitch. The head and line of balance at the moment of contact will be just in front of the left leg and the ball will be met as near as possible to the left leg. **All the best exponents of the stroke allow the ball to come very close to them before they play it: indeed they seem to meet it almost under their noses** (Fig. 25).

The left hand will retain control of the bat until the last possible moment, when the right hand will co-operate in turning the bat face for the deflection.

RUNNING BETWEEN THE WICKETS

Well-judged and keen running between the wickets is certain evidence of a well-coached and efficient team. The standard in most levels of cricket could be improved with tuition and practice. **Players should be made to realize that clear and sensible calling, quick running, and above all, quick turning are just as much part of good batsmanship as proper stroke playing,** and may easily determine the result of a match.

Such efficient running is often most unsettling to the fielding side which, unless well led and well disciplined, may easily be demoralized into misfielding and wild throwing with an expensive crop of overthrows. Moreover, the ability to call and run with safety quick, short singles from more or less defensive strokes, can upset a bowler, who is thereby denied the chance of bowling to a plan over a series of balls to a certain batsman.

Conversely, poor running not only loses runs but allows the field to be set deeper and so to cut off boundaries.

Finally, good running is enjoyable in itself – and especially to the spectators – reinforces the batsman's confidence, and generally keeps the game alive.

The chief points to be taught are:

Calling

1. Except when the ball goes behind the wicket, the striker must always call.
2. The call should be clear and decisive YES or NO or WAIT. Batsmen should be encouraged to make a habit of calling for every stroke.

3. For a hit that has passed the in-field and is obviously going some distance, the caller may, as he passes his partner, reinforce his first call of 'Yes' with 'Probably two' or 'Probably three'. But this is merely a warning and must always be followed by a definite second call.
4. For a second or subsequent run the call will always be made by the batsman who is running towards the wicket nearer to the fielder with, or in pursuit of, the ball.
5. A call, if refused, must be refused at once with a decisive 'No': once the batsmen have really started to run, they must go straight through at all costs.
6. Running for mis-fields is dangerous: there is a sound old saying 'never call for a mis-field unless there is a run and a half in it'.

Running

1. The non-striker should stand well wide of the return crease: he should generally hold his bat in his left hand (his right, if the bowler is bowling round the wicket) and, as the bowler delivers the ball but not before, should move a yard or a yard and a half down the pitch. He must always remember that his partner's run is as important as his own.
2. In running, the batsman (whether striker or non-striker) must always be prepared to change his bat from one hand to the other to make sure that he can watch the ball and not have to look over his shoulder in turning. The striker should always try to run down that side of the wicket from which the bowler is bowling: if he finds it necessary to run down the other side of the wicket it is the business of the non-striker to run well wide and outside him.
3. **Whenever there is any possibility, the batsmen must always be looking for more than one run for a stroke.** It is each man's job to complete the first run and turn as quickly as possible. Very many runs are lost, even in the highest class of cricket, by the tendency of batsmen to slow up over the last yard or two of their run-in, and half turn to see if there may be another run or not. The right order is RUN, TURN, CALL. But the batsmen must be sure to ground their bats beyond the popping crease before setting off for another run.
4. **In 'making good his ground' the batsman should ground his bat at least two yards short of the crease and run it in along the ground.** To dab the bat down at the end of the run is bad cricket and often leads to a run-out.

Running practice

The coach should give his side occasional systematic practice out in the middle: this may at times be dovetailed into the fielding practice described in another chapter.

His team will bat in pairs, properly padded and gloved, for five minutes or so each: the bowling will, of course, be adjusted to the purpose of the practice; it need not be in overs but, as in match fielding practice, there should at some time be a switch from one end to the other in order to familiarize the field with the light and surface on each side of the pitch.

In this practice the coach should emphasize the importance of being always on the look-out for the 'short single' from the stroke played slowly – indeed deliberately slowly – towards cover or extra-cover or to the left of mid-off and the right of mid-on: a stroke to either side of third-man offers a similar opportunity. In doing so, however, he will stress the relevance of the pace of the ground and the ability of the individual fielder. The call for a single for a ball played comparatively slowly to the left of cover may be perfectly sound if the ground is dead or if cover is slow, but suicidal on fast turf or if cover is a real specialist.

But whilst encouraging his batsmen to take every possible single and to turn ones into twos, and twos into threes, by quick turning and calling, the coach must realize that he is on dangerous ground, that run-stealing is heady wine, and that only experience can combine the art with security.

His last word must always be that a run is never worth the risk of a wicket.

PLAYING AN INNINGS

Though the teaching of a sound technique may be the coach's chief preoccupation, he will find that when it comes to match play, it must be reinforced by something else. It is one of the curious and fascinating things about cricket that a boy – or a man – may be far more or far less successful than his pure technique would seem to warrant, simply because he does, or does not, command the character and habit of mind that go to the playing of a long innings. One of the greatest of all English batsmen used to say 'Give me the batsman who makes runs: he is always in practice'. Every cricketer knows that a long innings in the middle is worth any number of nets.

Let us try then to get inside the mind of a young batsman and see how it can help him to play an innings. Let us suppose that he is No. 5 in the batting order: the first wicket falls and he loses no time in getting padded up, for nothing is more unsettling than to have to do this under pressure and then hurry out to the wicket with his mind in a turmoil. Padded up now and with bat and gloves close by, he can sit out in the sun, if there is any, to get accustomed to the light in which he will have to bat. He will watch the bowling carefully, trying to assess the particular problems that it may present, realizing perhaps that the medium-pace bowler at one end is coming off the pitch faster than his action would suggest, and that the slow bowler at the other, though giving the ball plenty of air, does not seem very easy to 'get at' on the half-volley. He will take a good look too at the placing of the field and its probable implications. Two slips and a gully, for instance, may suggest that a bowler is hoping to swing the ball away, a strong on-side field that he is trying to swing it in to the batsman.

Similarly he may conclude from what he sees that cover is a fine fielder with whom it would be dangerous to take a liberty, whereas there seems to be a safe run to third-man, who looks lethargic and who has to wind up to throw in, or to some fielder who is too deep.

Meanwhile, another wicket falls, and the returning batsman sits down beside him and begins to explain the rather obvious difficulty in which he has been at the wicket by an alarming picture of the bowling he has had to face. No. 5 will console himself with the reflection that, however difficult his friend may have found the bowiing, No. 1 is still there and seems to have been meeting it in comparative comfort! He knows too that the wicket is often a little lively in the first hour, but it is likely to be easier later on.

However, it is not long before No. 4, exhilarated after a shaky start by at last timing an off-drive perfectly, runs for a hit that goes straight and fast to cover's left hand and pays the penalty.

His turn has come. He does not wait for the returning batsman to reach the pavilion and walks out to the wicket, as a cricketer should, briskly but without hurry, reminding himself that after all, whoever is bowling, **batting consists of playing one ball at a time and that in playing it nothing matters so much as really watching it.** He has time, too, to reflect that No. 1 is now well in and going strong so that the more that he gets of the bowling the better, and that his own job is undoubtedly to play himself in quietly.

He takes guard, has one last look at the field to fix it in his mind, and then settles down to face a quick bowler with a gentle wind from the leg-side. The first two balls are some six inches outside the off stump, and fairly well up: he pushes forward and misses both. Far from being upset by this, he reflects that his luck must be in but that he would be unwise to tempt it further, and that for the next over or two he will do well to watch that type of ball go by.

An extra-fast straight and shorter ball finds him very nearly late with his back-stroke, and he remembers that at the start of an innings it is as well against quick bowling to pick the bat up early.

At the other end he sees his partner deal competently with an over from a slow left-hander and takes note that, though this man's stock ball spins away with the normal left-hander's break, the last ball of the over came in a little off the ground with his arm – he must watch the ball and play each one on its merits.

He has been in ten minutes and has still to make his first run, but this does not worry him at all, for what matters is not that he should 'break his duck', but that he should be still there and getting a sight of the ball. After all, it is the first 10 runs that take the most getting, and he has met and mastered the first attack. Meanwhile, how well his partner is playing, and how good it will be to see him get 50, especially as he has recently been out of luck and yet has never allowed it to get him down. What a satisfaction therefore it is when, by a quietly played push for a single off the first ball of the next over, he can give him the bowling and then by fast running and quick turning run three for a wide on-drive and see him safely home. And so to lunch.

After the interval, he reminds himself that no batsman can expect to go on exactly where he left off, but must play himself in again: in fact he must once again concentrate for all he is worth on watching the ball. Moreover, the wicket may have quickened a trifle and he must beware of being late to the fast bowler with whom they are sure to reopen the attack. He reflects too that, this being a one-day match, he must, if he is lucky enough to get going again, keep his eye on the clock and try to push on fast enough to give his captain a chance of a good declaration.

For a time all goes well: 30 runs are added and a strong off-drive to the boundary and a firm and a perfectly timed push wide of mid-on for two have reinforced his confidence, when suddenly things begin to happen at the other end. His partner has been dealing faithfully with a slow leg-break bowler, meeting him quick-footed and driving him firmly along the ground into the long-field; but, forgetting the bowler's obvious answer, he tries the same stroke to a ball pitched much wider of the off stump and spinning away, and is stumped. In the same bowler's next over No. 6, a dangerous but rather a scatterbrained hitter, omits to notice where deep-square-leg is standing and hits a high full pitch straight down his throat. Next ball his successor, a pawky player, plays back to a length ball which he expects to break from leg, but which, coming through straight with top-spin, has him l.b.w.

The whole balance of the game has swung round. With 6 wickets down, No. 5 is uncomfortably aware of a decided tail of a wicket-keeper and two bowlers who cannot be relied upon for much: in fact the only real batsman left is now leaving the pavilion, a player of real promise, but young and rather nervous.

He pushes tentatively forward at the two remaining balls of the slow bowler's over, misses them both, and is nearly stumped off the last. His partner is human enough to know what he is feeling, and cricketer enough to go down the wicket and give him some quiet advice and encouragement. This steadies the young player but the bowlers, elated by success, try for all they are worth to press home the attack and for several overs give nothing away.

Soon he realizes that time is slipping by and runs are needed now if there is to be a real chance of a win. His new partner cannot be expected to force the game, but he is a fine runner between the wickets, and he reflects that two or three singles an over can push the score along: so he sets out to get them, now steering a back-stroke just wide of mid-on, now pushing a forward stroke wide of mid-off's left hand, now chopping a ball to third-man, still obligingly on his heels. These tactics unsettle both bowlers and fielders: there is a four over-throw: the fast bowler trying to bowl too fast lets fly two very fast ones both of which are rank long-hops and are promptly hooked to the boundary, and No. 5 is past his 50 without even having thought about it.

The applause that greets it is sweet music indeed, but he has still a job to do, for stumps are not drawn until seven and his side still need some 30 runs more to make the declaration they would like. It is up to him to stay and get them, for nothing loses time as much as losing wickets and in any case the remaining batsmen may not get them at all.

The fast bowler has shot his bolt and has been replaced by the slow left-hander who, realizing that the wicket is not taking spin, is now concentrating on the ball that comes with his arm, with two short-legs and a forward mid-on. No. 5 realizes that these are a serious threat to his young partner's forward push: he determines to move them: after all, he will be hitting 'with the tide' and, if he looks at the ball and does not have a 'blind swipe', the truly hit on-drive that should follow will be unpleasant for the close fielders. His tactics succeed: a swinging hit nearly decapitates mid-on who retires discreetly, whilst a second leads to the forward-short-leg being dropped back on to the boundary, thus opening the way for both batsmen to play the swinger quietly for ones and twos into the on-side gap.

So the runs come and the captain waves from the pavilion to call his batsmen in: and very happily they return, the younger knowing that he has helped to hold the fort and is sure of his place in at least the next two matches, the older feeling that he has gained valuable experience in an innings to which mind and character have contributed as much as technique.

6

Captaincy

Captaincy wins matches and can lose them, but it can do more than that; it can make or mar a season, not only in terms of wins but in the general satisfaction and enjoyment which playing cricket should bring and which constitutes the real reason for playing it. Young captains can do a great deal not only for the teams they lead but for the cricket of their club or school in general. For their term of office they receive in trust its cricket tradition.

The method of their selection or nomination varies within wide limits, but there seems little to be said for the system whereby the senior player automatically succeeds to office. Experience is certainly an asset; so is personal prowess; but neither is so important as character, personality, enthusiasm and the capacity to think and learn about the game. **The sovereign virtue in a captain is unselfishness:** he must put others before himself.

Most young captains have a senior adviser or coach and they should miss no opportunity to avail themselves of his much greater experience. They will be wise to recognize that in seeking his guidance and support they will in no sense be impairing their own authority or prestige. They will welcome a discussion with him after each game and a tactical talk before the next one; sometimes the whole eleven will share in these. No captain can possibly anticipate all the demands that will be made on him, and the **best are those who realize from the start how much they have to learn.** Conversely, the coach will be most careful to avoid any appearance of dictation: his task is to anticipate the captain's problems, offer with tact suggestions for their solution, and progressively build up the captain's confidence both in the 'partnership' and in himself.

The captain must do all he can to achieve a well-balanced team. If he is a real leader, he must study each one of them as individuals, get to know their temperaments and how best to handle them both on and off the field. Nothing destroys morale more than a lack of communication between captain and players. When there are changes to be made in the team he must keep them fully informed, always ready with a kind word for those left out or omitted through injury, and a word of encouragement to the replacements. This will do much to build team spirit, the key to success.

Discipline is essential in any cricket team: ideally it should stem from a personal relationship in which confidence in and loyalty to the captain is automatic.

He should see that his team are well turned out, both as regards dress and equipment. Neglected boots may result in injury or lose a match.

He must be an optimist and inspire optimism in his side: he must show confidence in them in order that they may feel confidence in him: by personality and example he will get the best out of them. He must try to cultivate and show equanimity: however desperate the situation, his team must never be allowed to sense that their captain is 'rattled'. Encouragement is everything – it may be for a bowler when things are going wrong with him, for a fielder who has missed a catch, or for a young batsman faced with a crisis or out of form.

Criticism should always be constructive: slackness and bad behaviour merit and should get the rough side of the captain's tongue, and even then it is generally better to give it off the field than 'in the middle'.

A captain must know the Laws of Cricket and the 'Notes' that accompany them; this means some quite hard work. Few players really know them.

If there is a case for putting the other side in, he should allow himself sufficient time to consider all the pros and cons and to sound out the views of his leading players and perhaps his most likely wicket-taker. It is a basic rule that, if there is finally any doubt in his mind, he will elect to bat.

In all home matches he must, whenever possible, be on the ground to meet his opponents on their arrival and see them off at the end of the day. He will remember that he is a host and will do all that he can to entertain the visiting side; he will impress this too on his own team. He must make sure, before the toss, that he has exchanged teams with his opposite number and that the visitors are familiar with, and agreeable to, the 'custom of the ground' in such matters as hours of play, intervals, boundaries, etc.

Umpires, scorers and groundsmen will not fail to appreciate a word of thanks at the end of the match.

He must insist on punctuality. If his team is to field, he must ensure that his bowlers, especially the openers, have spent a few minutes 'loosening up': that there has been a short period of catching and throwing involving the wicket-keeper: that they are ready at least five minutes before the umpires go out so that they can take the field as a team. If his team is to bat, he will ensure that at least his first three in the order are 'padded up' in good time, and that his batsmen always cross on the field of play.

IN THE FIELD

The task of a captain becomes very much easier once he is the natural focus for his team's attention in the field. It should never be necessary to call out a name or to 'semaphore' for a change of position. If they are a well-knit team, they will always have an eye on their leader, ready to respond to unobtrusive signals.

Accurate positioning of the field is vital and he himself will form the habit of looking round at the start of every over: yet he must beware of being over fussy with small and often quite meaningless adjustments. His players must be made to realize that they can only change positions with his consent.

Before he takes the field he must have a clear idea in his head of his general tactical plan. He must have discussed with each bowler how he wants to dispose his field. He should also have thought out what adjustments will be necessary for each if a left-handed batsman comes in: many captains are apt to get in a serious tangle when faced with this problem.

In general the field will be placed for each bowler as the captain hopes he will, not as he fears he may, bowl. He must realize that the faster the ground, the deeper a fieldsman can stand and still save 'one'; the converse is equally true. He must avoid 'half-way places', too deep to save one and not deep enough to cut off the fours.

He will always try to keep as many fielders as possible in their 'specialist' places, but he will never allow any of his team to regard themselves as specialists pure and simple; they must all be prepared to field anywhere, though the slip fielders should be as constant as possible; he must protect his key bowlers from too much running and throwing.

He must keep his mind and his field flexible between attack and defence: this means watching the score, the clock and the individual batsman: with experience he will learn to assess one batsman as a probable back player, hooker and cutter, another as strong on the front foot.

He will always attack a new batsman and try to unsettle him, bringing in close fieldsmen for the catch whilst at the same time guarding against the single: he will remind his bowlers to make him play at every ball.

There are times when he will be attacking one batsman and defending against the other, even perhaps to the extent of giving the latter singles by opening out the field in order to get him away from the bowling.

In general, the better the pitch and the more set the batsmen appear to be, the more must a captain be prepared to experiment, especially with his slow bowlers, even at the cost of runs. If the batsmen really threaten to get on top, he must be decisive and tell his bowlers to bowl to a plan and set the appropriate field. The more difficult the pitch, the more he must rely on his best bowlers and set an attacking field: accuracy is now of the utmost importance.

At all costs he must try to retain the initiative and dictate to the batsmen, and not be dictated to. If he feels that the initiative is slipping from him, any move is better than no move: to change a bowler's end is often as good as a change of bowling: he must never let the game 'run on'.

The captain must maintain the flow of the game and he can do much to achieve this by seeing that his team has a good over rate. This does not mean that his bowlers should be asked to rush through their overs: on the other hand, it does mean that they should set off back to their mark as soon as the ball is 'dead' and that the fieldsmen, especially the slips and wicket-keeper, should not be allowed to dawdle across between overs. He himself can help in such ways as not taking undue time either talking to a bowler or re-arranging the field: once he has decided on a change of bowling he can give some thought to the new field during the overs preceding it.

Whilst the fast short-pitched ball, commonly called 'the bouncer', is a legitimate weapon of the fast bowler, the captain must see that it is used sparingly and never against unrecognized batsmen.

He will never allow irresponsible appeals from fielders who are not in a position to see: 'collective appealing' and gesticulations are contrary to the spirit of the game and he should strongly discourage them.

MANAGEMENT OF BOWLING

To make the best use of his bowling resources is one of the captain's most important and difficult tasks. A weak bowling side has to live by its wits – which means its captain's. He must first of all know his bowlers' capabilitites and temperaments and be able to handle them in the right way: much can be done by friendly discussion off the field to increase a bowler's grasp of tactics and to build up the morale necessary for what can be an arduous and at times a discouraging job: much, too, can be done on the field by suggestion and encouragement or a steadying word, and this is always easier if the captain is in close contact with the bowler, e.g. at mid-off. Such personal knowledge of his bowlers will often help a captain to sense after an over or two that X is 'feeling like it today' or that there is something wrong with Y's action, that his confidence is shaken, and that it will therefore be unwise to experiment with him for long.

But there will be much besides the personal equation of his bowlers to occupy the captain's mind. His bowling policy may sometimes be dictated – or at least influenced – by the direction of the wind and often by the state of the pitch which may vary from hour to hour and at times between one end and the other: for length is relative to the pace of the pitch, as well as to the pace of the bowler, and the captain will not hesitate if necessary to urge his bowlers to adjust their length accordingly. All the time he will be studying each batsman: for instance, the firm-footed or the nervy batsman may invite a slow bowler; the impatient dasher may be soon driven to suicide by sheer length; the 'flincher', if he so reveals himself, will be made to face up to pace.

But perhaps the most difficult problem a captain has to solve is between runs, wickets and time. Only experience can really help him to judge how long he can gamble for wickets with a spin bowler against a diminishing balance of runs and minutes: sometimes indeed whether he can risk at all the over or two which his spinner may need to find a length: whether his stock bowler is really pinning a batsman down or merely playing him in: how long to keep his fast bowlers on at a stretch, especially if the weather is hot, bearing in mind both their physique and temperament.

Success is a rare stimulant, and a bowler who feels himself on top does not readily feel tired, but a captain must beware of letting him have that extra over or two that may make a comeback so much more difficult.

Of course his tactics will be dictated by the resources at his disposal. If he has a fast bowler of any merit, he will certainly open with him, but he must be nursed so that he can be brought on again to attack new batsmen and especially the tail. At other end he will probably open with the bowler who is likely to make the best use of the new ball. The fast bowler should bowl down-wind, if there is any, and the other into it to help his swing. But if this opening attack does not seem to be causing much difficulty, the captain may well experiment by switching them to opposite ends.

Leg-break bowlers, if only they will keep the ball up and if they are supported by good fielding and wicket-keeping, are of immense value. It is always worth trying them against any batsman who looks like getting set, and a captain should soon be able to judge whether he 'knows the answer'. But such bowlers are apt to be expensive, especially on slow wickets, and it is generally important that the other end should be held as tight as possible with accuracy of length and direction.

A not uncommon mistake by captains is to run through all their possible change bowlers before reverting to their best bowlers: they must balance in their minds the need for adequate spells of rest against what is tactically the best attack against any given batsman or in face of any given problem of runs and time. Similarly, though they must, of course, play every match as a match to be won, they must think ahead through the season: a season's programme can be a heavy strain on young bowlers and it may sometimes be wise to take advantage of weak opponents, to rest the leading bowlers as much as possible and seize the chance of giving their understudies a run and perhaps the valuable encouragement of some wickets.

Perhaps the hallmark of a good tactical captain is his ability to keep an open mind and as the game evolves to be flexible in all his thinking.

THE BATTING ORDER AND DECLARATIONS

A captain should try to establish a settled batting order as early as possible in the season, for constant changes are unsettling to young batsmen. But there may be occasions when a change in order is desirable: for instance, he may wish to promote a stroke-player to catch up with the clock or to send in a left-hander to fulfil a special role. Not only must the captain be alert to such situations but should seek to give his batsmen as much warning as possible.

The opening pair are to some extent specialists: their first job is to 'see off' the new ball: to do so, experience of it as well as the right technique and the right temperament are important. But two purely defensive batsmen are not an ideal opening combination; it must never be forgotten that it is the aim of the batting side to wrest the initiative as early as possible from the bowlers, and to this end one of the openers at least should be a potential stroke-player.

A left-hander may be of particular value at the start of an innings: bowlers generally bowl less accurately to them in their opening overs, and the normally dangerous swing with the new ball which leaves the right-hander is less of a threat to a left-hander.

Nos. 3 and 4 may well be the two best batsmen in the side, ready, of course, if necessary, to hold the fort but with the strokes and the instinct of aggression to get on top and stay there: again, if one of them is a left-hander the side is lucky. Of Nos. 5 and 6 it is useful if one can act as a sheet-anchor, capable of redeeming an ugly situation by soundness of method and tenacity.

The captain should sit with his team for as much of their innings as possible; through his own experience and by closely watching the play he may often be able to help them, though he must never fuss them: they must feel that he is their leader just as much as when they are in the field. A word from him may do much to encourage a diffident or nervous batsman or to steady an excitable one. No batsman was ever the worse for being told, as he went out to bat, to look at the ball. **It is for the captain to tell his batsmen, according to the state of the match, when he wants them to try to force the pace and when to 'dig in'; they must never be left in doubt as to what his policy is.** The fall of a wicket often provides a chance of conveying that policy to the batsman in the middle through the in-going batsman. But as a rule the more the batsmen can be left to play their natural game the better, though when the wicket is really difficult and the bowling on top, it is likely that 'calculated hitting' would pay better than orthodox defence.

A great deal of nonsense is talked and written about declarations and the response to them. It is the business of every captain to try to win a match but, if he cannot do so, not to lose it. By all means let him err on the side of taking a chance in the pursuit of victory, but a so-called 'sporting declaration', which in fact gives the side that bats second a good chance of winning and the side that declares little or no chance of bowling them out in the time available, is not true cricket. The reasonable ratio of time to runs in a declaration diminishes with the increase of the target to be reached. The longer the journey, the better chance the bowlers have and the less likely that a fast pace of scoring can be consistently maintained. But the time ratio will also depend on the state of the wicket, the pace of the outfield and the captain's knowledge of his own bowling and the other team's batting resources. Having assessed all these factors and bearing in mind that 20 overs must be bowled in the last hour, the captain must base the timing of his declaration on the number of overs his team is likely to bowl.

In pursuing a declared total a captain will rarely be wise to alter his order and put his hitters in first, or even to instruct his openers to 'get on with it' at once. A good start is everything: the fall of early wickets in the premature pursuit of runs encourages the bowlers and at the same time makes the continuance of that pursuit all the more difficult. With wickets 'in the bank' the later batsmen can accelerate with a greater confidence or, if need be, 'put up the shutters' to avoid defeat. It is in this second stage of the innings that the captain may be justified in altering his order, bringing up his hitters, or holding back his left-hander because he may cause loss of time.

He will remind his team that from the first over they must be looking for the quick single, this in itself unsettles bowlers and fielders, and that quick and intelligent running between the wickets may well mean the winning of the match.

7

Learning by Watching

Though two of Wordsworth's nephews were the originators of the University cricket match, there is no reason to suppose that the poet had any interest in the game: yet he might have had cricket in mind when he wrote the line 'as if his whole vocation was endless imitation'. For whatever may be done by precept in the teaching of cricket, the coach will be wise to give his young players every possible opportunity of watching the first-class game, for they will instinctively and more readily imitate what they see than interpret, remember, and reproduce what they hear or read.

Let us then imagine him with a party of enthusiasts setting out for such a day's watching. Before he starts, or perhaps on the way, he will try to impress on them how much they can learn if only they will use their eyes, their imaginations, and later on their memories. He may well attempt a sketch of the leading players who will be on view and the particular excellencies which are to be looked for in each, recalling, if he can, some of their great achievements in order to instil a proper sense of respect and emulation.

On arriving at the ground and having taken their places, the party waits anxiously for the umpires, whose appearance may give the coach a chance to emphasize the vital importance of knowledgeable and attentive umpiring and to suggest that they should not take the umpires for granted but watch them and the signals they give.

Now comes the fielding side, looking, let us hope, like a proper team, well turned out, with clean boots and flannels following closely after their captain and obviously intent on business.

The placing of the field

The running commentary of the coach must, of course, be largely dictated by the incidents of play, but he may well try to concentrate at times on certain aspects of technique, in the hope that these may sink in and become part of his pupil's instinctive outlook on, and interest in, the game. He may first comment on the distribution of the field in relation both to the particular bowler and batsman concerned, and the presumed state of the pitch, no doubt calling attention to the way in which the field automatically sorts itself out at the start of the match with little appearance of direction from the captain.

His commentary may well be prefaced by a series of questions, designed to make his listeners use their eyes and think for themselves, for instance:

1. From the distribution of the field what do you think is the bowler's general plan of attack?
   e.g. (*a*) How can bowler A, opening with the new ball, justify having two slips and a gully and three men close in on the leg side?
   (*b*) Why does bowler B, an off-spinner, have no third-man, and why are his cover and mid-off so much straighter than for a leg-spinner?
   (*c*) Why for bowler C, a leg-spinner, do slip and gully stand unusually wide, and why is there a wide gap in the outfield between straight long-on and square-leg?
2. What alterations in field distribution are made between batsman A and batsman B and why? Why towards the end of the innings, when a new batsman joins a colleague with a good score to his credit, is the field so often adjusted for the last two balls of an over?
3. Why are mid-off, mid-on, extra-cover and cover, appreciably nearer in (or maybe further out) than when we watched a fortnight ago?
4. Why did forward-square-leg chase that ball instead of mid-on who was really nearer to its line?

The technique of fielding

Next, concentrating on technique, the coach may emphasize some of the following points:

1. The obvious and unremitting concentration of the slips and the close-in leg fields: their stillness and balance as the ball is bowled, with their weight forward on the front part of their feet.
2. The inward movement towards the batsmen of all the other fields as the ball is bowled.
3. The position of the fieldsman's head, body, hands and feet, both in attack and in defence.
4. The pace at which the ball is chased or at which the outfield comes in to 'save two'.
5. The balance for and the speed of the throw-in: its length – always full-pitch or long-hop to the wicket-keeper, or if to the bowler, the relay system so that he receives an easy catch and is never made to stoop.
6. The way in which, if there is a chance of a run-out at the bowler's end, mid-off or mid-on will get up to the wicket to take the return and to save the bowler's hands.
7. The automatic backing-up for the throw-in, with the backer-up always well away from the wicket.

Ian Botham. A remarkable stroke and demonstration of power: the forcing shot off the back foot back over the bowler's head *All-Sport/Adrian Murrell*

Test Match Scene. Viv Richards' full follow-through. The eyes of the bowler tell the whole story—a six over mid wicket *Patrick Eagar*

Other general reflections might well be:

1. The way in which a well-disciplined side will always keep their eyes on their captain who will never need to shout at them to secure their attention.
2. The ability of such a side to stick to it and keep its 'edge' even when it has been in the field for several hours and the score is reaching formidable proportions.
3. The obvious enjoyment that good fieldsmen get out of the game.
4. The number of runs that good fielding can save in any given hour's cricket, and the reinforcement it provides to the bowler and the curb and frustration it presents to the batsman.
5. The close attacking field (*a*) at the start of the innings, (*b*) when the bowlers are on top, (*c*) when time is short and the saving of runs not important.

Lessons from bowling

Switching his angle to the bowler and his craft, the coach may seek to drive home some of the following ideas:

1. The absolute regularity of the bowler's run-up, the rhythm of his delivery and his follow-through.
2. The way that all good bowlers make the batsman play at the new ball by bowling straight and keeping it well up: the way they attack each new batsman.
3. The use of the full width of the crease for altering the angle of attack.
4. Their skill in shutting up an end by bowling to their field: for this, control of direction, as well as of length, is vital.
5. The use that slow bowlers make of 'flight' and their readiness to be driven in the expectation that artifice of 'flight' and width may induce a mistake.
6. The slight variations of pace by medium-pace bowlers and the use by the fast bowler of an occasional 'yorker' and (or) extra-fast ball.

Lessons from batting

The following are some of the aspects of batting which careful watching may reveal and which the coach may do well to underline:

1. The ease, balance and stillness of the batsman's stance.
2. The straight high back-lift of the bat, and the opening of the bat face to cover-point.
3. The use of the feet, i.e. how far the good batsman moves his back foot to play back, and his front foot to play forward: how quickly and smoothly he moves out to drive, with the footwork never disturbing the sideways poise and balance of his body.

4. The way in which the head leads the feet and determines the player's balance.
5. The way the left shoulder and hand control the arc of every straight-bat stroke.
6. The position of the left shoulder and hip: the wider the ball to the off, the more does the batsman in the initial movement turn his back on the bowler.
7. The length of time the face of the bat moves down the line of the ball.
8. The way the ball on the leg stump or inside of the pads is played straight-batted, and 'down the line', with the head and left hand leading, and not hit right-handed and square.
9. The balance which is preserved in every stroke, even in hitting a rank long-hop or full-pitch to the boundary. Good batsmen never over-hit to the point of losing balance and so moving their heads.

There are of course, many other points of interest of a purely technical nature to rub in:

1. The way a new batsman will play himself in quietly until he has sized up the nature of the attack and of the pitch: he will not be seen playing defensive strokes at length balls outside the off stump: he will watch them go by.
2. The self-control and tenacity which refuse to be seduced by a couple of fine boundaries into taking a liberty with the next ball, and which regard the reaching of fifty not as an ultimate achievement, but rather as encouraging evidence that a long innings is on its way.
3. The readiness to play to the score or to the captain's orders without regard to personal average or interest.
4. The refusal to be 'rattled' when the bowlers are clearly on top and the batsman is, for the time being, clearly in difficulties.
5. The way in which one batsman who is well in will, if need be, nurse a new and less confident partner.

But from no aspect of batting can the young watcher be more sure of learning a valuable lesson than from the running between the wickets. He should be encouraged to notice:

1. The way the non-striker backs up.
2. The quickness and decision of the calling.
3. The way the bat is run-in along the ground at the full stretch of the arm.
4. The importance of completing the run and the turn as quickly as possible before the call for the second or third run is made.
5. The ease with which short singles can often be run, provided that both batsmen know and trust each other and that call and response are made at once.

LEARNING FROM TELEVISION

The extensive coverage of cricket on television has brought the game into the home and made it possible for many, who might otherwise have been unable, not only to see the experts but to study their methods at close quarters. Whilst some of the atmosphere of the big occasion may be lost to viewers, the confrontation between batsman and bowler can be clearly witnessed. This enables them to see in greater detail the finer points of technique, how much the ball is swinging or turning and the adjustment in the path of the bat needed to counter this movement. One important fact the observer should remember is that the close-up picture from behind the bowler has the apparent effect of slowing down the speed of the ball.

Only television can show the action replays at normal and slow speeds. These, used wisely, can be a great help to both coach and player when trying to determine or correct faults, and much more valuable than a still, or set of still, photographs. There is a saying that 'the camera cannot lie': this is true but what can be incorrect is the interpretation of the photograph. Many pictures are published suggesting that a batsman could have been given out l.b.w. from the position of his leg in relation to the ball: but had the path of the ball been seen, it would have been obvious that it was going to miss the wicket, thus justifying the umpire's decision. In fact the high standard of umpiring has been emphasized rather than deprecated by the television camera. Always remember that the umpire has no playback or slow-motion camera to help him, and look for the players who make his job easier by walking, when they know they are out.

8

Net Practice

Before being exposed to net practice, a boy or girl should have been initiated into the basic techniques of batting and bowling, perhaps through some form of Group Coaching. Nothing is more disheartening for a young bowler who is unable to bowl the ball down the net than to have to suffer the gibes and comments of his peers regarding his inadequate performance. Similarly, a batsman who seldom makes contact with the ball or who has no confidence and constantly backs away will not really profit from or enjoy his net session. Such players will also fail to give good net practice to other members and therefore the whole atmosphere of the session will be ruined.

During net practice the coach should instil into each player that, whilst cricket is essentially a team game, it is at the same time single combat – a bowler bowling and a batsman playing a single delivery. How the coach achieves this aim with his charges will vary according to their individual temperaments; one batsman with, say, a serious nature will only need reminding of his aims; another who is casual would require firm handling in order to make him concentrate seriously and so give of his best; yet another, who is timid and anxious, will produce his best results only when encouraged quietly. Ability to read a young cricketer's character is a very necessary part of the coach's armoury if he is to get the best out of his raw material.

The lay-out

Too much trouble cannot be taken to provide the best possible net pitches. Indeed, their condition is as important as that of the match ground, for on bad pitches batsmen can neither learn a correct method nor build up the confidence on which much of it depends, while bowlers are flattered by them and may get a rude awakening when they find themselves at work on a pitch that gives them no help.

Cricketers of all ages should be made to realize that they must themselves be prepared to do all they can to make their nets as good as possible. They should expect to have to roll the pitch before and after each practice: indeed, if the ground is being cut up, it pays to run a roller over it once or twice between each batsman's innings.

The net should be wide enough to allow the bowler to run off the pitch

during his follow-through. Far too many nets are extremely narrow or have guy ropes, pegs, etc., which have an adverse effect on the bowler by making him tend to follow-through down the pitch as he avoids them. Similarly, nets with little headroom or low tie bars might account for some slow bowlers who rarely flight a ball.

Whenever possible the lay-out of the net should allow enough space for a wicket-keeper to practise in the 'standing-up' position, providing other conditions are satisfactory.

The coach should be alert to and foresee problems arising from the fabric of the nets. Outdoor nets are mainly of heavy tarred string. Before practice commences the coach should ascertain that they have been erected satisfactorily, i.e. they will not fall down during the sessions; the bottoms have been pegged down securely so that they do not allow balls to be struck under the net or give so much under the impact of the ball that a batsman in an adjoining net is in danger of being struck. This latter danger is much more likely indoors with the frequently used and very popular lightweight artificial man-made fibre netting. There are several ways of preventing its movement, the best of which is to line the batsman's area of the net with heavy white canvas. Not only does this absorb the impact of the ball but it prevents the batsman being distracted by observing events in the adjoining net, or nets. Other safety aspects to be borne in mind are the repair of holes and attention to the pitch. If it is matting or similar material it needs to be stretched correctly and the pegs should not be left proud but driven well home.

The pitch markings, creases and stumps should all be set out as in a match, for this enables the bowler to adjust himself to the physical limitations laid down in the Laws. All too many bowlers ignore the creases during practice and find, to their cost, that in matches they frequently incur the penalty of a no-ball and the wrath of their captain.

Because of the lack of space and facilities at most schools and clubs, nets are invariably over-crowded. As a result, players become bored waiting their turn to bowl and start forming groups to talk, which creates a potentially dangerous situation as they are no longer concentrating on the batsman or the result of his activities. A maximum number of six can be profitably engaged at any one time in a net – one batting, one padding up, and four bowling. This number allows each bowler time to concentrate fully before bowling each ball. The player who is padding up should do so in an area designated as safe by the coach, i.e. to the rear or side of the net. All surplus equipment should be returned to or be available from this area.

Net discipline

Haphazard slip-shot net practice may well do more harm than good. **Boys must be made to realize that to make the best use of a net they must try for**

all they are worth, both for their own sake and for the sake of those that share it with them.

Before a session commences the coach should remind them that a net can be a dangerous place if safety precautions are not observed. Batsmen should always push the net away from them with the bat and drag balls out of it with a foot, so avoiding getting the head close to adjoining nets and putting themselves at risk to serious injury. Bowlers too should be made aware of the danger of balls from another net not only when close to the netting, but when returning from the crease to their bowling marks. In fact, anyone in the vicinity of the nets should keep his eye on the batsmen at all times and be prepared to react to balls being struck towards him.

A careful eye should be cast over the batsman to ensure that he has attired himself correctly, tidily and safely. All rings, watches, boxes of matches should be removed before batting, as painful and expensive results may be occasioned by a direct hit from the ball. It can readily be discerned whether laces are likely to come undone, straps are flapping or if a box has been forgotten in the rush to pad up. One other point, it looks much better to see trousers folded around the leg rather than tucked into socks.

Bowlers should mark out their runs correctly, provided space is available, which is not always possible at indoor nets, trying at all times to imagine that they are bowling at an opponent in the 'middle'. A net with a batsman needing and wanting practice is not the place to experiment or to learn to bowl a new type of ball. New types of delivery should be practised without a batsman and only perfected against him.

In a similar vein, batsmen should remember that although they cannot be out before their time is up they should treat each delivery as though they could be out and play them accordingly. A net which degenerates into a wild slogging match has a negative value for all participants, most of all for bowlers who are likely to become bored very quickly, when victims merely replace their stumps and carry on hitting.

Bowlers and batsmen should work together to ensure that the session runs smoothly and they give value to each other. The former should allow the batsman to settle down before commencing their run-up. To assist the bowlers, batsmen should lob the balls back after each complete round so that the bowlers do not have to bend for them. Some small children find difficulty in lobbing accurately with gloves on and in these circumstances it may be better for them to roll the balls back. Hitting the balls back with the bat should always be firmly discouraged whatever the age group concerned.

For maximum use of the time allotted for nets the order of batting should be made clear. In clubs this could well be the job of the captain to arrange, though in schools the coach will, no doubt, assume this responsibility. Several minutes before the next batsman is due in, the coach should send him to get padded up: this will allow him time to gather his concentration for the task ahead, and also give him a breather if he has had a tiring bowling stint.

Providing there is sufficient space and other conditions are satisfactory, there is no reason why wicket-keepers should not take advantage of net practice. It is most important, however, that the coach should observe the following points:

1. Wicket-keeping practice should be considered individually and whilst comment will be made to either batsman or bowler, his prime concern should be with the wicket-keeper.
2. No more than three bowlers (two are ideal) should be used and the conduct of the nets should be as previously described.
3. No bowler should be used to whom the wicket-keeper would normally stand back.
4. The wicket-keeper should be equipped exactly as he would be in a match: particular care should be taken to ensure that the correct protective equipment is worn.

Net practice is an excellent opportunity for a wicket-keeper to study and get to know the bowlers he would be required to 'take' in a match. Co-operation of the bowlers is essential and under the guidance of the coach they can be encouraged to bowl the type of delivery that will be most useful to the wicket-keeper's practice.

Practice behind a left-handed batsman is also very useful as, to the majority of wicket-keepers, the leg-side ball to the left-hander is one of the most difficult to 'take'.

Conduct of a net

Most coaches find it far more difficult to give real help to bowlers at a net than to batsmen and, as a result, it is certainly the case that the latter get more attention than the former. But the good coach will never let his bowlers feel that they are being taken for granted as mere adjuncts to net practice: he will be constantly watching their run-up, action and follow-through, stressing the importance of concentration, testing and challenging their accuracy by demands for, e.g., four successive balls just over a length and just outside the off stump, and stimulating their tactical sense by asking how, on observation of a given batsman's methods, they would propose to attack him in a match.

He will, of course, also be on the watch to see that a bowler does not get overtired, and if he detects this, will not hesitate to tell him to have a rest. This indeed is one of the greatest problems of net practice – and increasingly so as the season advances – to provide the batsmen with the best possible opposition and at the same time ensure that the bowlers are not over-worked: for bowlers get stale far more readily than batsmen, and they are the rarer and more precious cricket commodity.

The duration of each batsman's innings will, of course, depend on the time available for the net as a whole. Much can be done in ten minutes: few boys can bat profitably at a net for more than twenty, for it is, or should be, really hard work, and by the end of that time it is likely that, even if they are not beginning to tire physically, their concentration is on the ebb. So a batting session of fifteen minutes should prove most beneficial to the young batsman.

The batsman should bear in mind the sort of field that each different bowler might employ against him in a match. Beating an imaginary field is a good stimulus, but taken too far can detract from useful practice should the batsman fail to employ his repertoire of shots because he is trying to steer the ball instead of hitting it.

At the start of his net innings the batsman should play exactly as he would when he first goes in during a match, i.e. concentrate on playing himself in, getting the pace of the pitch and sizing up the bowlers opposed to him. He should, of course, not be discouraged from making strokes in his opening spell when the right ball comes along, but he must be brought to realize that a long-hop before he is sure of the pace of the pitch, or an apparent half-volley before he has mastered the bowler's flight, may not be the gift which it appears and which indeed it may well prove to be when he is well 'in'.

During this initial phase the bowlers will be urged to attack for all they are worth and be reminded that it is criminal not to make the batsman play at each ball, especially if it is swinging; that they must keep the ball up, and that every ball they bowl to which he can play back without hurrying, is 'one up' to him and 'one down' to them.

In this early part of any batsman's net, the coach should be trying to pick out the most basic faults and deciding how he can most effectively help. He should express appreciation of those strokes which deserve praise, whether they are of an attacking or defensive nature: similar favourable comments should be given to the bowler when his efforts warrant them. By taking up a position akin to that of an umpire, the coach can observe both bowler and batsman with the minimum of effort. However, there are times, particularly later in the season, as the coach gets to know his players, when it may be advantageous to observe and comment from other positions, e.g. behind the batsman, though of course remaining outside the net; he should always be within earshot.

In three or four minutes the coach should have decided what stroke he wishes to improve. With young players it might be more profitable to concentrate on improving the attacking shots which owing to lack of confidence the batsman hesitates to play in the middle. **The shot may well be played to balls which are thrown accurately by the coach, from not less than half-way down the pitch.** Far too many coaches perform this activity within such a short distance that the batsman has insufficient time to execute the stroke correctly, if at all. The resulting shots are usually bad ones with a marked lack of control which could result in the coach being injured by the ball.

Another fault of a great many coaches is that they will try to comment on every mistake they see and to eradicate all of them in one session. This merely confuses the inexperienced player, whose brain cannot cope with the flood of information being received, and frequently his performance will deteriorate rather than improve. The coach must also guard against taking a long time talking about the batsman's problems. A good demonstration by the coach, playing the ball, carefully watched by the batsman and the bowlers, who may have similar batting problems, can vividly illustrate in seconds something which would take much longer to put into words.

Having remedied the shot to his satisfaction the coach should now involve the bowlers by asking them to feed the stroke. This is good practice for the bowlers who will need to be able to bowl different lengths and directions, to suit individual pitches, left-handers, etc. in match conditions. After a further few minutes the coach may need to amplify or slightly alter his previous instructions before allowing the bowlers to revert to their normal deliveries and the batsman to play his usual game.

When circumstances permit the net should be brought to an exciting climax by setting the batsman a target that is within his range. A good batsman may have to get four runs off five balls if he is facing a strong attack, whereas his weaker brethren from the tail may have to score only one run without losing a wicket. It will be for the coach to decide whether a stroke would have penetrated the imaginary field and no doubt he will find himself engaged in enthusiastic banter regarding his decisions. However, if at the end of a long and tiring net session, interest has been sustained to that extent, he must be achieving his most important aim: cricket is exciting, stimulating, but above all fun.

9

The Choice and Care of Equipment

In the Long Room at Lord's there are preserved many bats of historic interest, including the curved and blackened veteran of the eighteenth century and the one used by Sir Donald Bradman on his last tour of England. Each in its time has been the personal and prized possession of some cricketer, and for every boy today, as he grows into the game, his bat is, or should be, part of his cricketing self, and its choice and care a matter of real concern.

In its selection a young cricketer will be wise to invite the advice of an experienced player. With bats now at a very high cost there is a natural temptation to recommend a youngster to choose a bat into which he will grow, but the price of such economy may be high, for his batting method may be seriously handicapped by using a bat which is either too big or too heavy. The special short-handled bat for young cricketers may be the solution to this problem.

Given that it is of the right size, the most important considerations are its balance and 'drive'. Balance is far more important than weight on the scales, and between two bats of the same weight there may be a vital difference in 'pick-up'. A well-balanced bat should lift easily and yet give the feeling that there is some 'body' in it as it comes into the stroke. The drive of the bat depends on the quality of its willow, the amount of wood in the driving part and the resilience of the handle. Given that the general weight and balance of the bat is right, the more wood there is in the blade the better. Most modern handles have the right resilience: this can readily be tested by placing the left hand at the top of the handle, the right hand at the bottom, and then, with the foot of the blade on the ground bringing a little weight of the body to bear, it should be possible to feel a definite give in the handle. The best willow, which comes from the heart of the tree, is straight grained: these grains may vary in number from five to twelve or even fifteen in the face of the blade: there is no golden rule but the more uniform the spacing of the grain the better. The only real test of a bat's drive is with a ball: the response of a real good blade is unmistakable in its liveliness, at once sweet and crisp.

The bat once selected, there is a good deal to be said for having its blade reinforced about an inch (25 millimetres) from the foot by a narrow strip of fine binding, for this is some insurance against the blade splitting, e.g.

in contact with a fast yorker, before it is really 'broken in'. The blade of a new bat should be oiled before use with a light bat oil, but care should be taken to keep the oil off the splice. Once a bat is driving well, the important thing is to keep the face clean with sandpaper and to confine the oiling to an occasional wipe-over with an oily rag. Bats must on no account be allowed to become wet; they should never be left to lie on damp turf, and, if rained on, should be wiped dry as soon as possible.

New bats must be 'broken in' discreetly: the best way to start is by knocking up an old ball on them. Cracks on the edge should be sealed at once with surgical tape; more serious damage may demand glueing and binding with twine, but this inevitably affects weight and pick-up. Rubber grips often tend to work loose, in which case they must be at once reglued, for a loose handle may very easily and fatally destroy a stroke.

Nowadays there is a variety of sizes of pads available and it should be possible for anyone of any age to be properly suited: the correct fitting of the knee is the acid test. Maximum protection must not be sought at the expense of comfort and mobility. Pad straps are generally made long and should be cut down so that only an inch or so will overlap the buckle: a cricketer should take proper pride in keeping his pads clean.

Whether in practice or in the middle, gloves should always be worn. There is a wide range of batting gloves manufactured today and choice is a matter of taste, though due regard should be given to the degree of protection. Some batsmen prefer those with a leather or cotton grip, others with the open palm, thus giving them the feel of the handle. A 'protector' is a great reinforcement to a batsman's confidence and may well save him from injury.

Footwear is a most important part of a cricketer's equipment, for it conditions the footwork and balance on which all bowling, batting and fielding depend. Rubber soles can only grip dry ground and for all conditions there is no substitute for properly studded shoes, or preferably light boots for bowlers, since they give better ankle support. Every cricketer who means business will keep a close watch on his studs to see that none are missing and they are not clogged up. Dirty boots are the sign of a slovenly cricketer. A pair of bootbags are very useful in keeping the dirt off other items of equipment.

A cricketer's outfit will, of course, be conditioned by his purse, but certain general aims may be suggested. A sweater is most desirable, above all for bowlers, who will be wise, even in warm weather, to put it on at the end of each bowling spell and, if it is at all cold, between overs. Many batsmen like to keep their sweaters on when they first go in: warmth is certainly essential if the muscles are to respond quickly and some find it also helps their nerves. But even if he is not making runs, a batsman very soon warms up at the crease and the sweater should then be discarded. Fielders, too, must keep warm and it is far better to go out in a sweater than to wish one had. A spare shirt should always be taken to a cricket match for if a player has really perspired, it will save him from stiffness. If he has an old pair of trousers he can use them for batting and so save his best pair for fielding, until in course of time they qualify for the other role.

Socks, though unseen, are not the least important part of the outfit and they should be thick: many players, especially bowlers, like to wear two pairs and chose their boots to fit accordingly: this certainly saves the feet on hard grounds and no one can do himself justice if his feet are blistered and sore. A change of socks, after a long spell in the field or a long innings, is wonderfully refreshing.

Some cricketers like to play in caps: those who prefer to play bare-headed should make certain that the hair is not so long as to get into their eyes.

In these days of mounting prices, cricket balls, whether private or club property, must more than ever be well looked after: they must never be allowed to lie out in the rain and if they do become wet or muddy after use at the nets or in fielding practice, they, and expecially their seams, should be cleared of all mud with a damp rag: they should then be wiped over with another that has a suspicion of oil on it and then allowed to dry naturally. It is wonderful how the life and the attractive appearance of a ball can be preserved with proper care and how soon neglect can transform it into something seamless, slippery and irresponsive.

A final word may be said on the winter storage of cricket equipment. Bats should be cleaned and lightly oiled before being put away and should be kept in as equable a temperature as possible. Boots and shoes, especially their soles, should be thoroughly cleaned.

It is most important as a safeguard against rotting that all netting, and matting where used, should be completely dried out before being stored. A slip-cradle must, of course, be brought under cover and a thin coating of oil smeared on the ribs.

10

Group Coaching—Why and How

It seems a fair assumption that those who really know anything about cricket – and about boys – will agree that it is a game worth playing, not only for the enjoyment it gives and for the friends it makes, but for the training it can and should provide for body, mind and character, and for the contribution which that training can make to happiness and good citizenship.

They will probably also agree that most small boys, given any opportunity, start by being eager to play it, but that all too few retain that early enthusiasm in face of the discouraging conditions with which they have to contend.

The root of their discouragement lies in the lack of playing facilities, the deplorable standard of many of them, and inadequate coaching in the basic skills of the game. To a great extent these two factors run together, for unless the practice pitches are reasonably true it is impossible to coach effectively, and on bad pitches the young batsman may well fail to profit by such coaching as he has had, whilst the bowler is flattered into thinking that he can dispense with it. A boy who is always dismissed as soon as he gets to the wicket will not long continue to play cricket.

All too few schools can command the resources to maintain turf pitches, whether match or practice, which will stand up to the wear and tear of a season's play. For the great majority the answer, especially for practice, would seem to lie in the artificial pitch. There is no need for the coach to be afraid that boys trained on such a surface will be at sea when they come to play on turf. There is, of course, a great difference between, for example, batting on concrete and a soft grass pitch, and a certain adjustment of technique and timing there must be, which only experience can give: but the fundamentals learned under favourable conditions will still hold good: indeed there is and can be no substitute for them and they alone can ensure the success in terms of runs and wickets which will sustain a boy's enthusiasm for the game and keep him playing it.

There still remains the problem of how these basic principles of the game can be taught at an early stage to all who are anxious to learn them. Of course, there is no substitute for individual coaching at a net and it is a very natural temptation for the coach to concentrate on the few boys most likely to profit by it. But he will be doing cricket a greater service and in the long run will reap a richer reward in the success of his teams, if he can, in the earlier stages, spread his coaching to cover all who want to play the game, and it is to meet this need that the technique of Group Coaching was evolved.

It is a matter of history that when, at the first conference on the M.C.C. Coaching Scheme, the idea of Group Coaching was first presented to the distinguished company of Test and County cricketers who attended, it was initially received with scepticism that bordered on incredulity. 'Teaching cricket by numbers', 'turning out robots', 'putting them all through a sausage machine': such were some of the terms of its early criticisms. But the proof of the pudding has been in the eating and today it is not only recognized as the only means by which the basic techniques can possibly be taught to all boys who wish to learn them in the conditions only too often still prevailing in many of our schools, but that it can also be of high value as a background and reinforcement of individual coaching, not merely for beginners, but for any young, or even not so young cricketer who is prepared to get down and work at the game.

The explanation is surely not far to seek. Batting, whether for a Test Match player or for a member of a junior school team, does consist of playing one ball at a time. To do this successfully a batsman must do three things: first, he must sight the ball; second, he must judge its length and decide what stroke he will play to it; and third, he must play that stroke correctly.

If to sight a cricket ball early and accurately is mainly a matter of the providential gift which we call 'ball sense', it should surely be assisted by correct positioning of the head and by general body balance in the stance. Stroke judgement, too, though partly a gift, is largely a matter of experience, though a coach can do something to help develop it in the nets and in discussion. But when we come to the actual stroke, we are concerned simply with a physical movement, the correct reflex response of the body to the brain's message. **This reflex response can only be achieved by constant practice: the body, in fact, must be 'grooved' to carry out automatically the right physical movement, and this is exactly what the activities of Group Coaching can and do achieve.** In them, for example, a batsman can in ten minutes play more off-drives to a ball dropped or tossed to the correct spot for that stroke than he might have the chance of playing in a whole afternoon of net practice. Thus gradually the stroke becomes grooved, and when next time out in the middle his mind telegraphs 'off-drive', his body will increasingly respond as it should.

The 'robot' criticism is frankly nonsense; batsmen will always vary according to their physical make-up, their natural gifts, their personal temperament: one's approach will be instinctively aggressive, another's defensive: one will naturally tend to play off the front foot and with plenty of top hand, another off the back with the right hand largely in control:

one will be ready and able to 'go down the pitch', another will tend to play 'on the crease', but whatever their natural resources and their basic approach, Group Coaching can help them to make the most of them.

Many of the distinguished players who have attended courses for the Advanced Coaching Certificate formerly run by the M.C.C. and now by the National Cricket Association have volunteered their conviction that not only is group practice of high value as basic training for stroke production but that they themselves have even profited by it in their own play. Similar tribute is paid by many of those who have attended the consistently over-subscribed N.C.A. courses for schoolmasters; they have found Group Coaching pays a real dividend at all levels of their school cricket, not only in terms of analysis, understanding and technique, but also in active enjoyment and sense of achievement.

The principles, whether of batting, bowling or fielding, which the coach should teach, have been set forth in the various chapters of this book, and it is here assumed that he has tried to study and master them. **He must all along try to explain 'why' as well as 'how',** e.g. why the bat must be as long as possible on the line of the ball; why the position of the head and left shoulder, the movement of the feet, the control by the left hand, matter in batting; why the bowler must keep sideways, use his body and follow-through; why the fielder must stoop early and keep his head down – and so on.

He should encourage his boys to ask questions in order to ensure that they really understand both the 'how' and the 'why'. In time he may even be able to single out one or two who can help him as 'junior coaches': incidentally, the ability in a young cricketer to spot and to analyse another's faults in technique can be a great asset in improving his own.

As in all class-instruction there must be discipline and concentration and the coach must try to be as 'hundred-eyed as Argus' to mark what is done amiss. But he must always remember that for the young 'practice' is to some extent an unsatisfactory preliminary to 'the real thing', and he must ring the changes between, on the one hand, spells of 'stroke-grooving' and training in the pure technique of bowling and fielding and, on the other, competitions and match practice on the lines that will later be suggested. **Above all there must be good humour and encouragement** and at the end of every session the coach and his boys should feel that they have really 'got somewhere'.

EQUIPMENT

Group Coaching demands a certain amount of equipment, but not more than the initiative of games masters and the co-operation of boys should be able to provide. The following are suggestions which can no doubt be improved and extended with experience.

Bats

A number of bats or bat shapes are necessary and it is very important that there should be a sufficient variety of sizes to cater for all their users: **no boy can hope to derive benefit from practice, even from group practice without a ball, if he is using too big a bat.**

The following table records the dimensions and average weight of the various sizes of bats which are manufactured and suggests the approximate age for which each will normally be found suitable, though, of course, the determining factor in each case will be height and strength. A serviceable test is a boy's ability to swing and control the bat reasonably with the top hand alone. It is always better for the bat to be too light than too heavy.

DIMENSIONS OF BATS

Size of bat	Length of bat		Length of handle		Width of blade		Weight			Height of user	
	cm	in.	cm	in.	cm	in.	g	lb	oz	cm	ft in.
FULL SIZE	88·90	35	30·48	12	10·79	4¼	1020·58	2	4	175·26 plus	5′ 9″ plus
SHORT HANDLE	86·36	34	27·94	11	10·79	4¼	1020·58	2	4	170·18– 175·26	5′ 7″– 5′ 9″
HARROW	86·36	34	27·94	11	10·79	4¼	992·23	2	3	165·10– 170·18	5′ 5″– 5′ 7″
6	83·82	33	27·31	10¾	10·16	4	963·88/ 935·53	2	2/1	157·48– 165·10	5′ 2″– 5′ 5″
5	80·01	31½	27·31	10¾	10·16	4	907·18	2	0	154·94– 157·48	5′ 1″– 5′ 2″
4	76·83	30¼	26·67	10½	9·84	3⅞	694·565	1	8½	139·70– 154·94	4′ 7″– 5′ 1″
3	66·04	26	22·86	9	8·25	3¼	510·29	1	2	below 139·70	below 4′ 7″

Cricket balls

Proper cricket balls should when possible always be used for bowling and batting practice, but their life on hard surfaces tends to be short and there are a number of relatively cheap and efficient types of composition balls on the market. It is important that small boys should not be allowed to practise or play with the full-sized ball; a smaller and lighter ball 134·66 grams (4¾ ounces) is now available. For indoor practice tennis balls are normally used for all strokes. However, there are occasions when it may

Group coaching. The 'coil' position

Fielding. Eyes on the ball, hands well cupped *All-Sport/Simon Bruty*

Teaching the forward defensive stroke to enthusiastic beginners *All-Sport/Simon Bruty*

Teaching the pull stroke, with a soft ball. Note the eyes firmly on the ball, but the head must later move outside the line *All-Sport/Simon Bruty*

be more prudent to use the plastic 'Gamester' ball. These can be hit very hard without danger to the players or the fabric of the building.

A useful aid for demonstration and diagnostic purposes has been the recent development of a two-coloured ball, one half red, one half white.

The wicket

Several portable wickets will be needed: these are best provided in the form of a wooden base 27·94 cm by 7·62 cm by 7·62 cm (11 in. by 3 in. by 3 in.) into which stumps are inserted, or a plywood board of the correct width and height: if the stumps are painted on the latter so much the better. The base can profitably be stabilized by two metal bars, approximately 45·72 cm (18 in.) long, 3·81 cm ($1\frac{1}{2}$ in.) wide and 0·64 cm ($\frac{1}{4}$ in.) thick, secured at right-angles to its length: but this is not necessary. Wickets can also usefully be chalked or painted on convenient walls.

The pitch

Ideally, the pitch should always be measured out accurately, using a chain or tape measure. However, a length of cord or string with knots at 1·22 m (4 ft), 18·90 m (62 ft), and 20·12 m (66 ft) for the creases and pitch length, is a cheap and useful substitute.

Length targets

These are best provided in the form of thin tin plates, at least 91·44 cm by 60·96 cm (3 ft by 2 ft): the tin, when struck, makes a satisfactory noise. Alternatively, plywood can be used, or the target can be chalked on the gymnasium floor or playground by filling in the area within the plywood frame.

It is also advisable to have some tape or string rectangles 5 m by 1·5 m (17 ft by 5 ft), 4 m by 1 m (13 ft by $3\frac{1}{4}$ ft), 3 m by 1 m (10 ft by $3\frac{1}{4}$ ft), for the use during Proficiency Award testing.

Catching aids

Slip-cradles, of course, are excellent, but they are expensive and heavy to move about. A possible improvisation is the ordinary curved-topped dustbin can, which with a tennis ball can provide very useful practice for quick reaction to catches at close range. The fielders should form a circle, standing at just more than full arm stretch from each other and with a radius of 3 or 4 paces from the bin. The new plastic spring-board screen provides excellent and enjoyable practice.

There is no substitute for constant practice and the coach should try to provide all the facilities he can for it, whether in the form of an adequate supply of bats and balls readily available, or permanent marks in the shape of wickets and length-targets at which they can bowl.

BATTING

When commencing to teach batting to youngsters who are absolute beginners, the coach should always remember that **a good demonstration provides more information and is, in most cases, more easily understood than a talk of several minutes' duration.** Boys cannot concentrate for long periods of time and the coach should keep his introduction to a minimum so that activity commences as quickly as possible.

It is very easy to forget something of importance when teaching and to diminish the chance of this, a set order or routine should always be used.

The first thing the coach will do is to divide the children into groups of five, six or seven according to space and the stroke to be practised, and number them within the groups. The coach should then decide into which area the ball is to be played and so arrange it that the children will be able to see the demonstration clearly without the danger of being struck by the ball. **Every stroke commences with the batsman waiting to sight the ball from his position on the crease,** therefore, the coach should draw a crease on the ground with chalk: sometimes this is not possible when working indoors, but there are adhesive coloured tapes which can be used instead. The popping crease should consist of a straight line, with a short line drawn at right-angles pointing to the middle stump to give an indication of where the wicket should be. To assist the batsman further the coach should also draw in the positions of the feet in the normal stance, i.e. heels equally spaced just either side of the popping (batting) crease. As he does this he should explain the reason for each mark or line.

The coach is now ready to play the stroke which he is about to teach without a ball. The length of the ball should be made clear and the stroke performed. Attention should be paid to the position of the feet at the end of the stroke and the position of them drawn on the ground.

Now is the moment to set up a group so that the coach can demonsrtate the stroke with a ball and all the children can learn the organization of groups for batting. Each member of the group will have been previously given a number and the coach will use one group to set out the apparatus and markings as the model for all.

Duties within the group

1. Batsman – collects a bat, chalk, marks out the crease and foot positions.

2. Bowler – marks out target for the ball and his bowling position.
3. Feeder – collects balls and keeps a supply ready for the bowler.
4. } Fielders – collect skittles, measure out target area, field within it,
5. } return balls to feeder.
6. Wicket-keeper – when required, extra fielder or recorder for Proficiency Awards.

Group Coaching practice and instruction

Having set up his demonstration group and taking the place of No. 1, the batsman, **the coach should inform the bowler to say 'Bat-up' and wait for the batsman to lift the bat to show he is ready, before delivering the ball.** This is vitally important as it enables the batsman to settle himself before each stroke and, therefore, concentrate properly. If this point is not stressed most children will deliver the ball far too frequently and much of the value of the practice will be lost.

As soon as the coach has given a good demonstration of a selected stroke he should emphasize one or two features of the stroke and then set the groups working in previously selected areas. Each batsman should have about six attempts at the stroke and then the group rotates so that in a short time they have all experienced the movement required. Only then should the coach start to impart a little more information; this again should be done by demonstration. The reason for this is that boys cannot assimilate large amounts of information at one time. By stressing only one or two points they can concentrate more fully and so perform the required movements.

In these early stages only brief mention will have been made of grip, stance or back-lift, for nothing puts off children more than time so spent. This must not be interpreted as meaning these points are unimportant for this is not true. The coach is more concerned with getting them to hit a ball as quickly as possible in order to further interest and give the individual a sense of achievement. The coach should stress that **all strokes start with a back-lift** hence the instruction from the bowler of 'Bat-up'. As for the grip, if the bats are the correct size and weight, the majority of children will learn to hold them correctly fairly quickly. This can, of course, be talked about during the explanation of each stroke as it is introduced. At a later stage, when they have progressed, it will be necessary to get them in pairs and with one acting as a coach, following a detailed description and demonstration of the grip, stance and back-lift, pick out and correct the faults in each other.

When involved in Group Coaching the coach must ensure that he does not concentrate on individuals to the exclusion of the group. He should look for common faults and draw the attention of everyone to these faults and their correction. **It is always important to state why a particular action**

is wrong and the advantage to be gained by performing a stroke in the correct manner. He must encourage the children by reminding them that instant success is not always forthcoming, but with practice, especially in their own time, everyone can improve. This improvement will be made most quickly by those who treat each ball as though it was being bowled in a match and consequently really concentrate on playing it accordingly.

The coach now faces the task of choosing the first stroke he is going to teach. Some coaches would have no hesitation in advising that the first stroke should be the forward defensive stroke and there are several points in favour of this decision. It is a stroke which gives the ball less chance to move off the pitch to beat the bat and boys are less likely to be late in playing the stroke.

However, there are possibly more valid reasons for choosing the hit to leg off the back foot. Very few young bowlers bowl a full or good length and therefore, the ball tends to bounce rather high. They also find difficulty in bowling straight, thus a cross-batted stroke is frequently used. Hitting to leg is the most natural and vigorous way of dealing with the shorter ball, which provides enjoyment with each successful attempt. All the coach has to do in effect is to improve this natural swing of the bat to produce the required stroke.

The hit to leg off the back foot

He will now divide the children into groups of six, each child being given a number within his group: he should inform them that he is going to demonstrate how to hit a short pitched ball to leg. He should then draw the crease and stance markings informing them that this is the job of the No. 1 in each group. The stroke is now played without a ball and the coach should draw attention to the way both feet have moved back and are pointing forward about shoulder width apart as for the pull stroke. These new positions of the feet should also be drawn as guides.

The coach should now instruct the No. 2 of the demonstration group to walk 5 paces away from the crease straight down an imaginary pitch and then draw an arrow pointing at the batsman before walking another 5 paces to draw a circle from which the No. 2 will deliver the ball. Whilst No. 2 is doing this No. 3 will have collected some tennis balls and should now be standing adjacent to No. 2. Depending on the space available, Nos. 4 and 5 will have been pacing out the target area into which No. 1, the batsman, will attempt to play the ball. If space is limited they will measure out 10 paces along the popping crease to the leg side and then turn at right-angles to place a skittle, rounders post, stump, etc. $2\frac{1}{2}$ paces in front of the crease. After a further 5 paces, the second skittle is placed on the ground and Nos. 4 and 5 field between the two skittles, i.e. within the target area. If ample space is available the above distances may be doubled. For this practice No. 6 acts as wicket-keeper.

The coach should now inform the bowler to throw downwards to try to hit the head of the arrow so that the ball will bounce thigh high as it arrives at the batsman. It may be necessary for tall children to kneel on one knee if too high a bounce is obtained from a standing position. Before throwing the ball, the bowler should call out 'Bat-up' and not deliver the

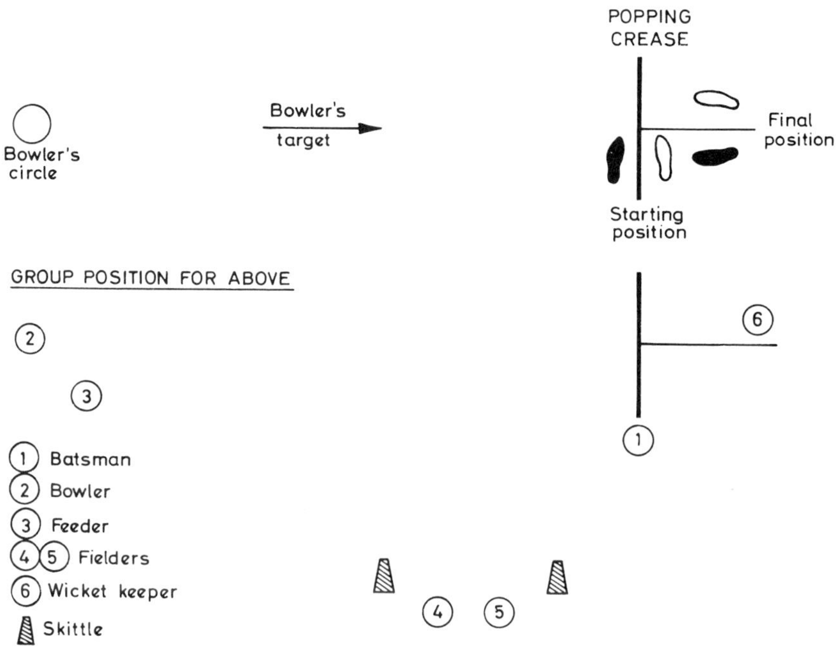

Fig. 1. Chalk marks for hit to leg off back foot

ball until the batsman has raised his bat as demonstrated by the coach. It should also be stressed that **the ball should be struck downwards so that it bounces before it passes through the markers of the target area.**

The coach should now play the stroke having previously ensured that he can be watched from a safe position. After the completed demonstration the coach should give out the three things he will be looking for: **high back-lift, stepping back on to the marked position, hitting the ball downwards.**

These points will be quite sufficient for the children to try to concentrate on for a first attempt. Indeed, the coach may find that some will only get into the correct position, 'chest on', at the completion of the stroke by starting in that position.

The other groups should now set up the equipment for the practice and commence, changing round after, say, six attempts. After everyone has had experience of the stroke the coach should introduce his next point, which could be in the form of a question: 'Why are so many of you hitting the ball in the air?' If the correct answer is not suggested he should inform them and give a quick demonstration showing how they must lean forward to prevent the ball going in the air. The groups then continue practising and the coach can visit each group in turn giving help where necessary.

At every demonstration the coach should repeat each previously made instruction so that, as the session progresses, a complete guide to the stroke is built up. This helps to reinforce the learning process without overloading or confusing. The coach should at all times be alert to the amount of information that can be assimilated in a short space of time and not be afraid to change to a different activity if he senses that the group as a whole is tired or bored with the practice being undertaken.

Hit to leg off the front foot

For this stroke which is played to a full-pitch outside the leg stump the basic layout remains much the same as for the stroke off the back foot previously described. The coach should, as before, after demonstration, first mark out the crease and foot positions. This time the front foot position will be on or just outside the line of the imaginary leg stump. If space is rather limited the ball can be played against a wall so that the fielders, Nos. 4 and 5 in the groups, can field the ball safely on the off-side, after it has rebounded. Note that the feeder No. 3 will receive balls from the fielders on the off-side so he too stands on that side.

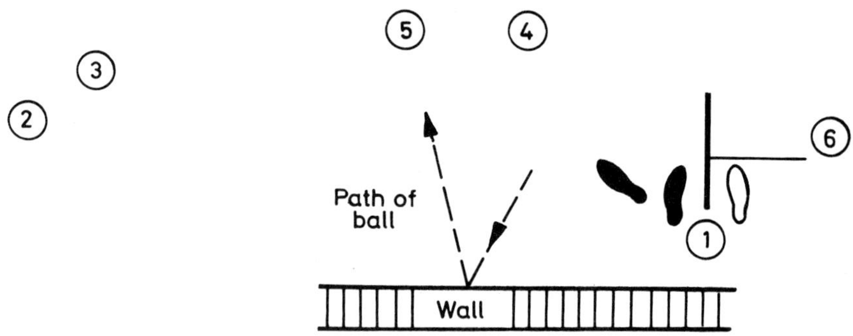

Fig. 2. Chalk marks for hit to leg off front foot

Having given the call 'Bat-up' the bowler lobs the ball so that it should land on the thigh of the batsman's outstretched front leg if he misses it with the bat. After or during his demonstration the coach should list initially no more than three items on which to concentrate: **high back-lift, lean forward, hit the ball downwards.**

He should then bring in the other points, one or two at a time, after all have had experience of the stroke.

The back-stroke

If the coach has taught his pupils the two cross-batted shots previously, they will be able to score runs off the more wayward bowling, but find they are lacking when better balls are bowled which require a defensive stroke. Once more it may be necessary to remind coaches that, although many youngsters are coached on comparatively flat surfaces, playgrounds, indoor

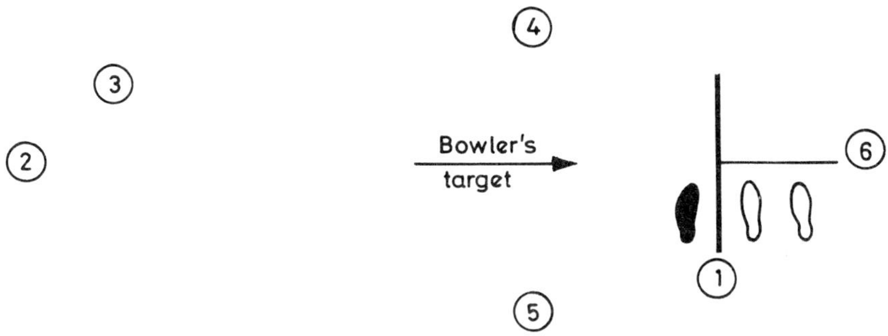

Fig. 3. Chalk marks for back stroke in defence

sports halls, etc., the majority do not play their cricket on such true surfaces and are, therefore, reluctant to play forward. A coach should always be aware of and ready to incorporate the movements which his pupils are likely to make into the preliminaries of those he is trying to teach. Since they have already the inclination to move backwards it would seem sensible to channel this inclination at an early stage, into the commencement of a recognized stroke, such as the back defensive.

The coach should mark out a crease and initial foot positions before demonstrating the stroke without the ball. Emphasis should be made of the fact that he has stepped back and across to play the short pitched ball, which would have bowled him if it had not been played with a straight bat. The position of the back foot, pointing behind or at most parallel with the popping crease, should be chalked on the ground. Because this is a defensive stroke, Nos. 4 and 5 in the group will have no target area to mark out, so the coach will position them one on the off and the other on the leg side to try and catch him as he plays his demonstration stroke with the ball. In all other ways the group is as for the hit to leg off the back foot with the bowler trying to skim the ball at the batsman, so that it does not bounce much above knee high.

The initial points the coach should stress are: **the back foot moves back, straight back-lift and down swing of the bat, no follow-through as this is a defensive stroke.**

The diagram shows the disposition of a group of six. This practice can also be performed by three, a bowler, batsman and fielder if sufficient equipment and space are available.

The forward stroke

Before starting to teach this stroke the coach should have included a session on grip, stance and back-lift, since the downward swing of the bat in a vertical plane between wicket and wicket, is of great importance in this stroke.

The class should be split into groups of three or four and for this practice No. 3 is a fielder. Once more the coach should draw his crease and stance foot marks before informing the class that he is going to play a defensive stroke, on the front foot, to a ball of good length, or one that seems to pitch too close to the batsman for him to have time to play a stroke off the back foot. He should play the stroke without the ball to establish the position of his front foot which he should then mark. This should be in line with leg and middle stumps and a comfortable stride forward for a straight ball. About 30 centimetres (1 foot) in front of this foot mark and about 8 centimetres (3 inches) to the off-side of it the bowler should draw an arrow pointing towards the batsman to serve as a target on to which the ball will be lobbed underhand from about 6 to 8 paces away. Nos. 3 and 4 from the group field on the off and on sides to try to catch the ball from the stroke. When playing the stroke the coach should remind the class that they must imagine they are trying to avoid getting out in a match and, if possible, play the ball, so that the fielders have to come to the batsman to pick it up. His initial coaching points should be: **straight back-lift, lead with head and shoulders, no follow-through.**

As before, everyone should have a given number of attempts and then rotate within the group, before further information is imparted.

In all Group Coaching accurate service is essential and the boys should be informed not to play a stroke if the ball is considerably off target. In fact there are occasions when the service may require almost as much practice as the stroke itself.

There are slight variations in this stroke to balls pitched on the off and leg sides. These require slight adjustments of the markings for the front foot and bowler's target. To generalize, lean towards the pitch of the ball and the foot should automatically move in the required and necessary direction.

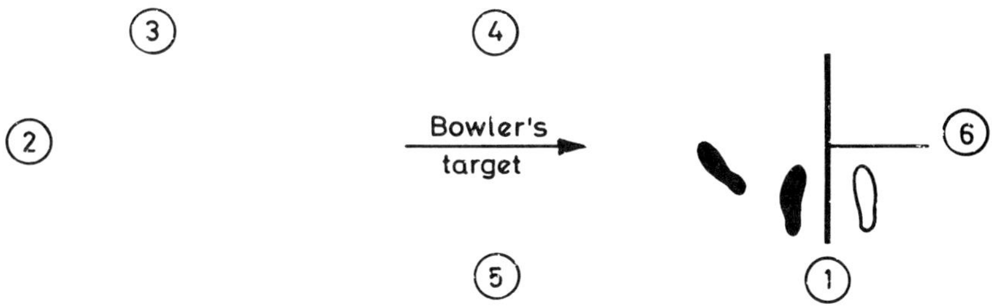

Fig. 4. Chalk marks for forward stroke

The drives

The drive, whether straight, to the off or to the on, is really only an extension and acceleration of the forward stroke: once a player has learnt how to play forward, he should be taught to drive, for until he can do so he can be immobilized by the bowler who keeps the ball well up to him. Moreover, it is the most exhilarating stroke in cricket and no part of group practice will pay a bigger dividend in enjoyment and in a feeling of achievement.

The coach should divide the class into groups of six as in earlier strokes and draw his crease, together with the stance markings. Perhaps the off-drive is fractionally easier to play than the other drives so he should introduce this stroke first. The stroke should be demonstrated without the ball and the position of the front foot, which should have moved a comfortable stride forwards and to the off side, marked. An arc, from the toe of the front foot extending for about a foot towards the crease on the off side, should be drawn as a target for and by the bowler. The bowler stands to the off side of the batsman, at such a distance that when his arm is extended horizontally the ball will drop from the eye level of the batsman on to the arc, which he has drawn.

Meanwhile Nos. 4 and 5 will have marked out the target area: if space allows this will be 10 paces wide at a distance of 20 paces from the batsman or as previously 5 paces at a distance of 10 paces (Fig. 5).

For this practice No. 6 can be extra fielder or recorder.

The coach must stress that **the ball is dropped following the call of 'Bat-up' and not thrown or flicked as it is released.** It should be struck on the second half-volley, i.e. immediately after the second bounce.

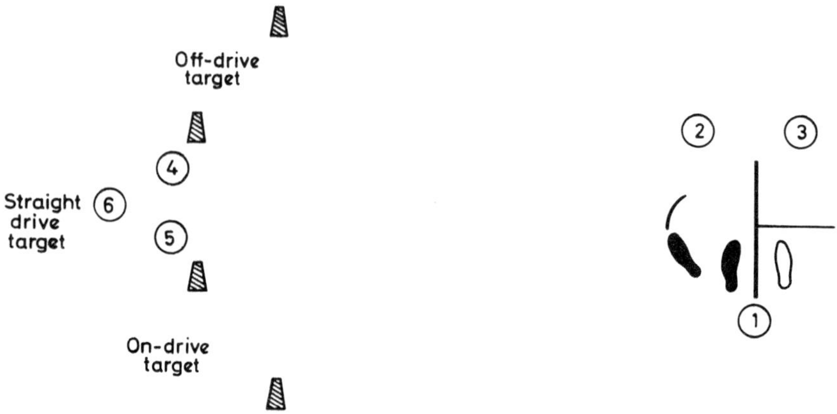

Fig. 5. Chalk marks for drives

He should emphasize the high straight back-lift, the lead of head and left shoulder and follow-through up the line during his demonstration, before quickly getting the children working. Once every child has had experience of the stroke the other important points should be introduced.

This practice can also be performed from one end of a gymnasium, playground, etc. with all the fielders at the opposite end to the batsman, bowlers and feeders. This is a fairly safe way of coaching larger and stronger pupils as **there is a possibility of injury if fielders approach within less than 9 metres (10 yards) of the bat.**

By altering the angle of the crease it is possible to have the ball struck in the same direction despite changing the required stroke from, say, off-drive to the on-drive (*see* Fig. 6).

Balls are now struck in this direction for all the drives.

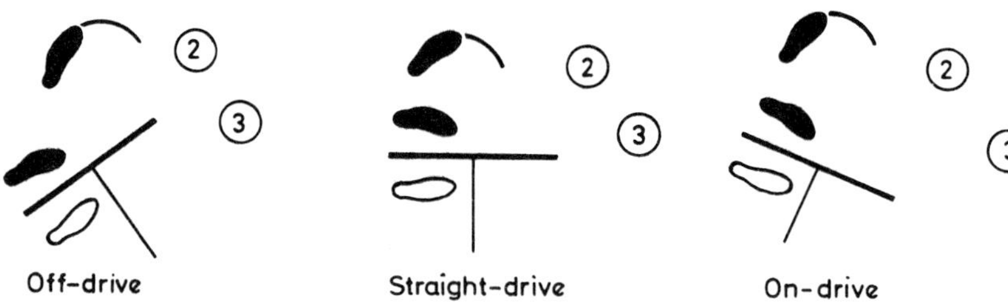

Fig. 6. Crease alignment for playing all the drives in one direction

Practice for moving out to drive can also be usefully performed by having the bowler stand about two paces in front of the batsman and dropping the ball from a higher position to give the batsman more time to 'glide' out to the ball. If 'Gamester' or plastic 'Airflow' balls are available, a great deal of enjoyment and useful practice can be obtained by lobbing these balls into the air for the batsman to move out and play. Because these balls soon lose impetus this practice can be carried out quite safely across the width of a normal gymnasium. However, as with all practices, the coach must ensure that the bowlers and batsman are spaced, so that bats can be swung without the likelihood of anyone being struck.

Tennis courts with nets can, when available, be used for a more advanced form of coaching. Tennis balls are lobbed from one side of the net to a batsman who should be some 8 to 10 paces from the net. This has the advantage of demanding from the batsman some judgement of the flight of the ball, giving a feeling that this is a more directly related practice for batsmanship.

Attacking back-strokes

Many children find these rather difficult strokes to perfect in the net, but they are ones which will rapidly improve with Group Coaching. The layout of the crease and foot markings are as for the back defensive stroke, but the batsman should aim to play these into the same target areas as for the drives. The ideal height of the ball for these strokes is about knee high and the bowler should aim to throw the ball low and fast.

The coach should stress the need to keep sideways on so that the bat travels along the line of the ball and the intended stroke, not across it. Other vital points are to aim to keep the ball down and not to try to hit the ball too hard.

'Gamester' balls can be used for this practice, but there is much more satisfaction to the batsman if the more solid contact with a tennis ball is experienced.

The cut

This is the most difficult stroke to coach in Group Coaching because a correct stroke can only be played if the ball is served at the correct height, distance and speed. However, it is a very pleasurable practice and much satisfaction can be gained from it.

The coach should stress the necessity for moving the back foot back and across, together with the need to come down on top of the ball to try to avoid being caught.

For the purpose of this practice it helps the bowler to throw in the correct direction if the wicket-keeper stands about a pace to the off side of the batsman. The target arrow should be about 4 to 5 paces from the batsman and about 48 centimetres (18 inches) to the off side. Left-handed

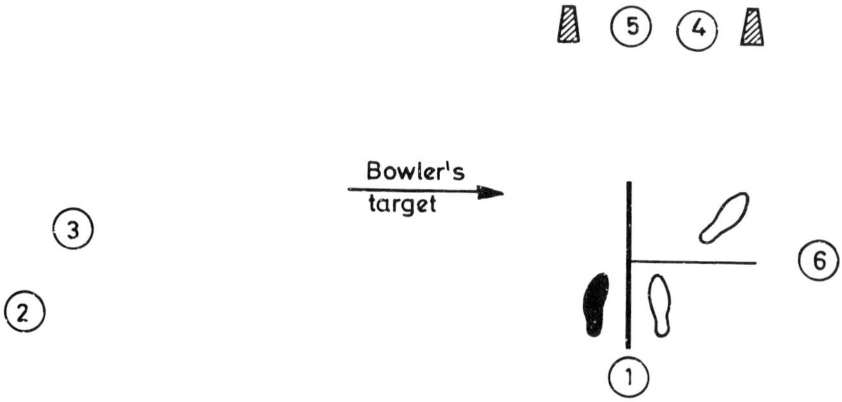

Fig. 7. Chalk marks for cuts

throwers may find it helps them to throw across the batsman if they stand rather more on the leg side.

In all the above practices the chalk marks of foot positions and target arrows are only guides. Small children may have to stand closer to some targets and larger children further away. Bowlers may have to alter their positions from standing to kneeling if they are obtaining too much bounce from a particular ball or surface.

The coach must not take too long when talking about a particular stroke but get the groups working as quickly as possible. **Only when they have had experience of those movements of which the coach is talking will they begin to fully comprehend his explanation.** Occasionally it may help to reinforce his teaching if the children 'shadow' the stroke with their bats as a class. Providing the coach keeps the left-handers on his left and the right-handers on his right, when facing them, he can quickly pick out those whose movements do not conform with the correct ones and adjust them.

BOWLING

Whereas a good deal of Group Coaching practice in batting may seem to young players removed from the 'real thing', this is much less true of bowling. But here too **the foundations must be laid by explanation, demonstration and repetition of the correct bowling action.**

To discover how great a task he has in hand the coach should divide his group into pairs and without any tuition at all get them to bowl to each other. Alternatively he may, if space is restricted, ask them to run and demonstrate their own bowling actions without a ball. From this brief observation he should note those pupils who will require extra help, e.g. those bowling off the wrong foot, the hoppers, etc. and also those who can be used as models at a later stage.

The pairs should face each other across the room or if outside about 15 to 20 paces apart. It is a good teaching point to ensure that left-arm bowlers are on the left of the coach as he faces them as this enables them to see him more easily. The coach should then demonstrate Position 2 of the Basic Action, 'the coil', and get everyone to adopt this position. **This is the only occasion when children are held for any length of time in a static position during the teaching of bowling.** From 'the coil' they should swing the front arm out and down towards their partner whilst at the same time the bowling arm swings completely round, starting from the chin. The coach should emphasize the following facts:

1. **Look behind the high front arm at your partner with the back slightly arched.**
2. **Lean back, away from your partner, and then swing forward towards him, swing the arms – no jerking.**

Fig. 8. The Basic Action: position 2

Immediately the coach is satisfied that 'the coil' position and the swinging action of the arms are correct he should introduce a ball into the activity. Only two points need to be made at this stage:

1. **The ball should be held in the fingers and not in the palm of the hand.**
2. **The ball should hit the ground before reaching his partner.**

This is all the information necessary to start children bowling. Other information – high arm action, follow-through, etc. – is brought in as soon as they can cope with it. Never forget, too much information in a short space of time confuses and little valuable work can be done if the children have tired of or are bored with an activity.

Once children can deliver a ball correctly, enjoyable and useful practice can be done by making them bowl from 'the coil' position in games which can be played in the gym or on the playground.

The next step is to introduce the run-up. It is vitally important to get youngsters to understand that **the function of the run-up is merely to enable a bowler to arrive at the crease balanced and with sufficient momentum to complete the bowling action successfully.** The bowler with the speedier approach is not always the one who bowls the faster ball.

When teaching the run-up the coach should first establish which is the correct take-off foot for everyone in order to try to avoid the development of hoppers or those who bowl off the wrong foot. An easy way of doing this is to line the children up and ask them to raise their bowling arm. If they are instructed to stamp the foot, which is on the same side of the body, until it tingles, they will all be able to differentiate between their feet. The 'non-tingling' foot is the take-off foot and the tingling foot the one on which to land, thus obviating the terms right and left which can lead to confusion for left-arm bowlers.

The coach should now demonstrate 'The Bound', described as a jump in the Bowling chapter, by running 2 or 3 strides before taking off and landing. As he takes off, both arms should be raised in the air, and he should draw attention to the fact that his take-off foot is the 'non-tingling' one. The children should now perform this activity several times across the area while the coach observes very carefully to make sure that only the left-arm bowlers take off from the right foot.

The next step is to introduce a 90° turn whilst in the air so that the landing will be made with feet at right-angles to the line of travel. This is a very important movement as it enables the bowler to get sideways on to the batsman. Following the successful copying of this action, the class will move on to landing in 'the coil' position where they should pause before running on. To hold 'the coil' position for a second or two it is necessary to lean well back from the intended direction of the ball. It should be stressed that prior to landing in this position their run-up should be controlled and unhurried.

Now the teaching of the run-up is complete and the whole bowling action should be practised – run, bound, land in 'coil', bowl. This practice should be performed with the ball, allowing plenty of space and with the accent on perfecting the action rather than on accuracy, particularly if the children are rather young. At all times encouragement for getting some part of the action correct should be forthcoming from the coach to promote enthusiasm for an activity in which some will find little reward at first.

The more able should now be required to demonstrate a degree of control by bowling at targets marked on the ground in front of a wicket. However, **the size of the target must be large enough for the average**

beginner to hit frequently rather than rarely. Too many coaches mark out targets which are so small that the poorer bowler becomes so discouraged with failure that he rapidly loses any wish to participate and improve. For real beginners and juniors, a target area of 5 metres long by 1·5 metres wide (17 by 5 feet) immediately in front of the crease (as used in the First Test of the Proficiency Awards Scheme – *see* Chapter 11), should be employed. As the bowlers improve then this area can be diminished accordingly, until for the real experts something approaching 0·9 by 0·6 metres (3 feet by 2 feet) is utilized.

There are various competitive points systems for bowling which can be used to stimulate interest. For beginners, points should be scored for hitting a length target and also the wickets. When the bowlers have gained some degree of success they should be encouraged to try to bowl a particular type of ball and obtain another point if the ball moves in the correct manner. It is very important that children who are trying to become spin bowlers should practise their spinning technique as soon as their bowling action is satisfactory. It is of little use to be able to bowl slowly a line and length but not be able to pitch the ball when trying to spin it. Target positions need to be varied so that each type of bowler learns to pitch the ball in the correct area for the ball to be most effective, e.g. off-spinners must pitch outside or on the off stump. Faster bowlers will have their target a greater distance from the batsman than slower bowlers. One further consideration is the allowance the coach makes for the age or physique of his bowlers with regard to the pitch length. As a general rule those under 11 should bowl on pitches of 18 yards (16·44 metres), 12- to 13-year-olds on those of 20 yards (18·28 metres), and 14 years plus on those of a full 22 yards (20·12 metres).

A greater degree of realism is introduced if some object (e.g. dustbin) is placed on the crease, an inch or two outside the leg stump. This simulates a batsman and helps some bowlers to find their length by using it as a reference point.

FIELDING

In Chapter 2 the basic technique of fielding has been analysed and some fielding and catching activities performed with cricket balls were mentioned. Before reaching that stage **all children should first have been taught to catch using soft balls so that confidence is built up.**

Close catching is best taught in pairs, opposite each other some 5 to 6 paces apart, using a tennis ball. The coach should demonstrate the readiness position and get the children to copy him. He should always stress that in catching, the fingers are pointed at right-angles to the line of direction of the ball whenever possible, as this lessens the chance of injury to them. It is important to give the reasons why they should give with the ball and show what is likely to happen if they do not.

The children should now practise catching with the accent being made on the style and level of success. When a high rate of success is achieved this is the time to put the skill under stress to discover if the technique is sound. This is done quite simply by counting the number of catches made in a period of time and then trying to increase the number in a similar time. This brings in the element of competition and helps to make practice more enjoyable.

Other practices such as catching against walls are very useful and can be varied quite easily. Beginners can work in pairs side by side facing the wall and catching alternately a ball bounced off the wall. Later, one stands behind the other and throws the ball against the wall so that the catcher, who is facing the wall, does not know when or where the ball is to be thrown. This demands more concentration from the catcher to achieve a high rate of success.

Team games such as Spry, Corner Spry or Scotch Handball provide other purposeful and useful practice.

High catching can also be taught in a similar manner indoors although it is rather difficult to make more catches in a short space of time. It is possible to record how many catches can be made before one partner makes a mistake, and then try to improve the number. Outside, very good practice can be obtained by hitting tennis balls into the air with a tennis racquet.

Teaching children to throw correctly is one vital part of fielding that is often neglected and taken for granted. Throwing is a skill and needs proper tuition as much as any other facet of cricket. They should be taught to throw overarm to hit a target chalked on the ground midway between them when spaced either across a gym or out on the playground. It should be stressed that they throw downwards in order to develop a good follow-through. This practice can be developed into competitions such as who can get the most hits out of ten attempts or in a given period of time. Team games or competitions knocking skittles over or driving a football towards your opponent's 'goal line' are ways of making throwing practice fun. A word of caution is necessary at this point. Shoulders are susceptible to injury caused by throwing, therefore prolonged throwing practice is not to be recommended.

The playground is an ideal place to learn to stop a ball. It is little use trying to practise this skill if the ball is bouncing erratically on poor turf. The coach should demonstrate the long barrier method of stopping the ball, stressing the fact that he does not look up until the ball is safely gathered in his hands. Indoors it is then only necessary to move into a throwing position before rolling the ball back across the room for the partner to perform the same action. Outside, if space permits, the throw to an acting wicket-keeper can be incorporated. Attacking fielding and retrieving the ball are both activities which can also be practised in this manner and provide a good deal of exercise as well as useful skill training in this situation. Any teacher or coach who has no field available should still be able to give valuable fielding practices provided he can find a level piece of playground or time in the gymnasium to attempt some of the above suggested practices.

WICKET-KEEPING

Wicket-keeping is another facet of cricket which lends itself to simple practice on a hard level surface. Since no special equipment is needed for beginners, **every child should be involved in the exercises to ensure that no potentially good wicket-keeper is overlooked.**

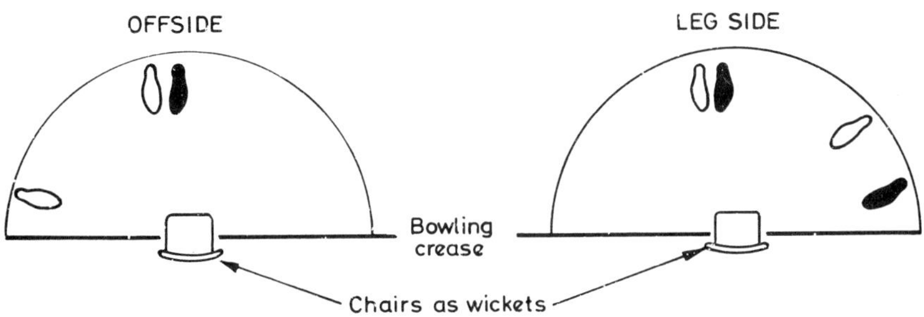

Fig. 9. Chalk marks for position of wicket-keeper's feet

For the purposes of demonstration and practice a chair is an adequate substitute for a wicket. Behind this the coach should draw a semi-circle, radius 1 good stride (*see* Fig. 9), to act as a guide for the feet. Having adopted and explained his stance (*see* page 21) for keeping to a right-arm medium-pace or slow bowler, bowling over the wicket, he should demonstrate how to take a straight ball thrown from about 10 paces in front of the wicket, to bounce about bail high, just outside the off stump. He should emphasize that he **stays down until he is sure of the line of the ball: his hands give with the ball and then takes it back to the stumps.**

The children should set out chairs, wickets, etc., draw the semi-circle and practise in pairs, using a tennis ball, one throwing and one keeping until the basic movements are performed skilfully.

The next step is for the coach to demonstrate the taking of a ball wider to the off, requiring a movement of the feet. **He should stress the turning inwards of the right foot and the fact that he has moved forward.** An incorrect demonstration moving the foot backwards and not turning the toes towards the stumps will show very clearly that a stumping is almost, if not completely, impossible from this position. He may decide to chalk footmarks on the floor to draw attention to the placing of the feet. After further practice, which could incorporate bowling practice if sufficient space is available, the coach should demonstrate the leg-side technique, once again stressing the inward turn of the feet so enabling the possibility of a stumping. The practices can be made more difficult and realistic by a batsman who plays at the ball but deliberately misses it on nearly all occasions.

INTRODUCTORY GAMES

Many young children are not ready to play full eleven-a-side games, but should be encouraged to participate more fully in games of lesser numbers with the accent on enjoyment and activity. As they become more skilful and mature, so the demands of the games become greater.

Non-stop or continuous cricket

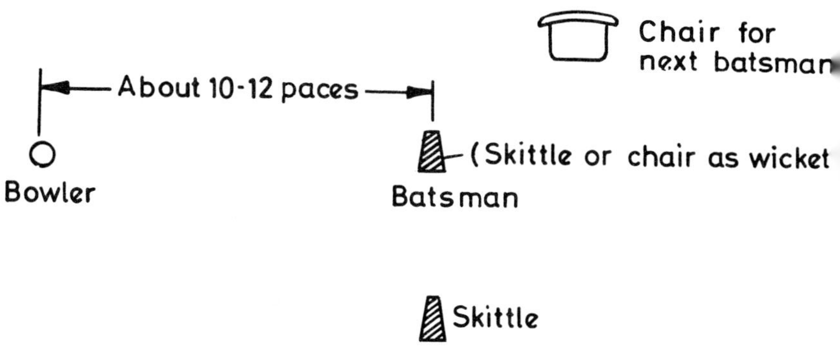

This is an excellent game which provides plenty of activity and excitement. The bowler bowls underarm to hit the wicket after one bounce. Whenever the batsman hits the ball with a small or suitable bat he must run round the skittle. If he returns to his batting position he scores a run. He can only be out bowled or caught, but the bowler bowls as soon as the ball is returned to him whether or not the batsman has completed his run. The incoming batsman must not leave the chair until the batsman is out. When all the side is out the innings is complete and the fielding side bat. It is advisable for the coach or teacher to bowl in early matches for both sides.

This is a game in which the accent is on teamwork in the field and engenders the sense of urgency in the fielding side. If time is short it can be made harder for the batsman to remain in, by moving the skittle further away from the wicket.

Stoolball

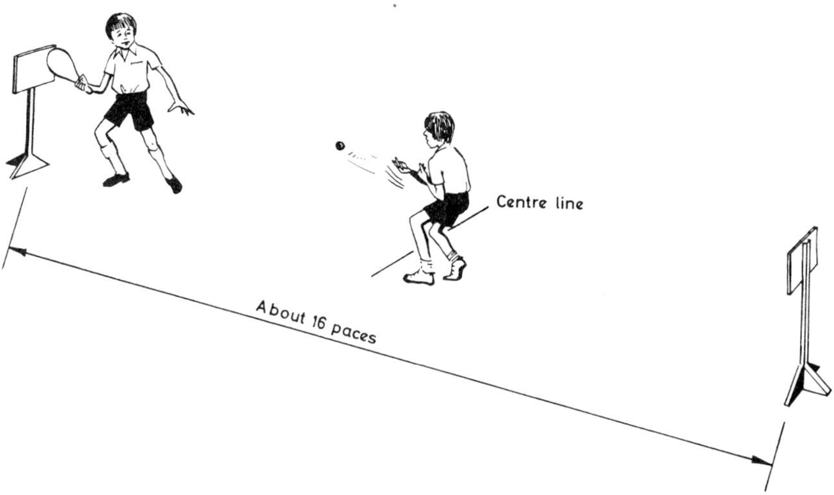

This game introduces running between wickets, the concept of wide balls and unfair deliveries, i.e. no-balls, and is played in pairs. Special stoolball bats and balls are available but improvisation is less expensive.

The pitch is about 16 paces long and the bowler bowls underarm from half-way to try to hit a target about a foot square at shoulder height. (The back of a school chair is quite a satisfactory substitute.) After 6 balls, an over, the bowler becomes wicket-keeper and vice versa, so that the bowling is now directed at the other target. The batsmen, who bat for 2 overs, can be out, bowled, caught or run-out. To make their ground they must have the bat behind the target before the fielding side hit the front of the target with the ball. If each pair's runs are divided by the number of wickets they lose, an average will be found and the pair with the best average wins. Children can also learn to umpire for themselves in this game and everyone should have a turn. It is easy to devise a work card or system of changes to accommodate various numbers and a suggested system for 6 pairs is shown in Fig. 10.

Circular cricket

This game can be played as a single wicket form of cricket with children changing round as in the suggested way for stoolball or in pairs. The number of overs each pair of batsmen receive will be dictated by the time available. Each pair of batsmen should receive the same number of balls, irrespective of how many times they are out, as this is also a game which is won by the side with the best average.

As long as the pair who pad up and score are the next pair to bat the system can be added to according to space available, e.g. a pair to field deep on the leg side, etc.

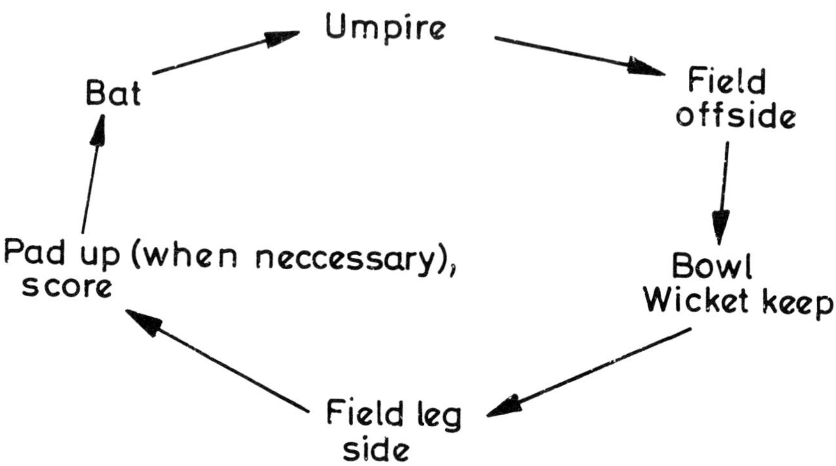

Fig. 10. Work card for Stoolball or Circular Cricket

Pairs 8-a-side cricket

In this game the rules are as for the game of cricket, with the exception that each pair of batsmen bat for 4 overs in 16-over games and 5 overs in 20-over games. Everyone must bowl except the wicket-keeper and no one may bowl more than 3 or 4 overs, depending on the total overs to be bowled. Each side starts with one wicket down, to ensure a proper average. The advantage of these games is that if a child makes a mistake he can atone for it. Also, he participates fully and is not just a fielder or number eleven, who feels that he is just there to make up the team for the benefit of the other members.

The organization of a cricket games lesson

Each lesson should have an aim. This aim should be to introduce, revise or improve a particular skill and should occupy a fairly early part of the lesson when the children are fresh. The lesson itself should be divided into three main sections:

1. Warm-up
2. Main theme
3. Activity.

Warm-up activities should be vigorous to stimulate the children and capture their interest. The quality of any subsequent practice depends on the involvement and concentration established in this section. Many fielding activities, e.g. chasing and returning, attacking fielding, etc., come into this category.

The main theme may consist of two parts – the first, a revision of a known skill, the second may be a completely new skill or it may be a continuation of the skill that was revised, e.g. 'the coil' followed by the introduction of the 'bound'.

The final activity depending on time and space available may be a competition for points based on a skill taught during the lesson, e.g. bowling at targets, driving into a target area. Then again a complete change may be required if the coach or teacher thinks the youngsters have become bored.

Two games of continuous cricket could be played simultaneously in the average gymnasium within 5 to 10 minutes. As children become more proficient, the demands of the game must increase so that they obtain more satisfaction. The better ones will want to move from stoolball to circular or pairs cricket. These games take longer and are more suitable for the longer games period.

It should be the aim of all involved in games teaching to provide a continuous, varied and satisfying set of activities for everyone. Only in this manner can enthusiasm for practice be stimulated. As the season goes on, less time need be directed to skills and more time to match play or practice; for without such games being organized for them, they will see little profit in trying to improve themselves.

11

The National Cricket Association Proficiency Awards Scheme

This Proficiency Awards Scheme has been designed to provide a series of incentives for boys and girls to learn, practise and enjoy the skills of the game; those skills which are so necessary for success.

The Award Scheme has three grades, First Test, Second Test and Final Test. To gain an award a youngster must obtain sufficient points from tests on batting, bowling or wicket-keeping, fielding and also be able to answer questions on cricket generally. The First Test pass level of 40 per cent should be well within the capability of the average 10- or 11-year-old; the Second Test level of 60 per cent for those aged about 13; the Final Test pass mark of 75 per cent demands rather more than average performance and only those who can produce a high level of success will achieve it.

Many sports have introduced similar schemes, but any award scheme used incorrectly may prove a hindrance rather than an aid to teachers and coaches. All batting tests are based on the actual practices and group organization as set out within it. Provided that a teacher or coach has adopted the Group Coaching techniques, the only extra item of organization needed will be to supply each group with a pencil and record sheet. The children note the number of successful strokes achieved. This record sheet will then not only inform the teacher or coach of those who have achieved sufficient points to pass a test, but will also provide valuable information as to the progress of each individual.

Any school, cricket club or other organized body may arrange tests for their members and any adult from that body may act as examiner for the First and Second Tests. For a Final Test, the examiner must hold one of the M.C.C. or Cricket Council's Coaching Awards or have been nominated by the local County Cricket Club, Schools Cricket Association or Local Education Authority. These tests are ideal for cricket clubs and organizations who have access to playgrounds, indoor facilities and good grass playing fields.

Further information, entry forms, record sheets, etc. can be obtained from The Secretary, National Cricket Association, Lord's Cricket Ground, London NW8 8QN.

12

Fitness for Cricket

Few games make the varied, physical demands upon a player as does cricket, especially when played at the highest levels. A fast bowler may be asked to bowl flat out for up to two hours: a slip fielder may not have to field a ball all day and then with all his muscles cold explode to propel himself through the air to make a diving catch: batsmen too have the problems of forcing themselves to concentrate and take quick singles, handicapped by pads, following an arduous fielding session. To achieve success a high degree of a special sort of fitness is required.

Fortunately for the majority of those who play cricket as a recreation, it is possible to play and enjoy the game with little or no special training. However, the more dedicated, keenly competitive and younger players will derive more pleasure and satisfaction from the game, if they have taken the trouble to achieve a state of fitness suitable for the effort they may be called upon to produce in the type of cricket which they play.

Everyone needs an individual schedule of exercises to make certain that maximum benefit is obtained from time spent in training. The player should not be content merely to repeat a schedule but keep increasing the demands made on his body. In the early part of the year the schedule should consist mainly of stamina and strength exercises with some time spent on ensuring that mobility exercises are not forgotten. Later, as the season approaches and commences, exercises more directly related to cricket have a greater value, e.g. the various non-stop fielding activities, net bowling, etc.

All ball games make great demands on the legs and cricket is no exception. If one considers what is required of the muscles of the legs for acceleration, braking, turning and just walking into position during a match it will come as no surprise to learn that various kinds of running should form the basis of early training. Many people think that to go for a jog trot and gradually increase the distance as they become slightly fitter is quite good enough. There are far better ways of becoming fitter and they take less time than the above. **All running should be aimed at increasing the distance covered in a given time, reducing the time for a given distance or reducing the rest period between each activity.**

The following running activities can be recommended for rapidly increasing fitness: obviously they cannot all be attempted in the same training session.

Up-hill running

For this exercise the steeper the slope and the more loose the surface, the better – a sand dune is ideal – for these factors increase the demands made on the body. Each individual should run up the slope as fast as possible for 20 seconds and mark the spot which he has reached. His work load will be to try to reach the mark in 25 seconds on six consecutive attempts. A recovery time of 2 to 3 minutes should be taken whilst walking back to the start.

Interval work

This type of training can be performed on the playing field around the boundary or even on the side of the road. As before the player should sprint from a fixed point marking or making a mental note of his distance covered in 20 seconds. His target will be to sprint this distance six times in, say, 25 seconds each attempt, following a recovery period whilst walking back to the start.

Note that in the above activities initial progress is achieved by reducing the time taken in covering the target distance. Once this has been done the recovery interval should be decreased so that as fitness is improved the demands made upon the body are increased to ensure further improvement.

Distance running

Many people enjoy 'jogging' but steady rhythmical running for long periods does not rapidly increase fitness nor does such activity occur in ball games. If there is an area of open country near at hand a weekly run lasting at least 20 minutes can be very valuable. However, the pace should be varied frequently and maximum benefit will be gained if slopes are attacked and different soils or surfaces can be included on the way. Steady plodding runs, such as ten times round the pitch, should be avoided.

Shuttle sprinting

This exercise is very useful for general fitness and particularly for batsmen. Two wickets or markers should be placed about 30 paces apart. Players jog to the first wicket and then sprint to the other one. Having passed it they should slow down, turn and then jog back before sprinting between the wickets on the way back. Eight sprints are undertaken before a 3- to 4-minute rest. The sprints are then repeated twice with the same recovery period between them. As fitness increases progress should be maintained by increasing the number of sprints from eight to ten and later decreasing the recovery period to 2 or 3 minutes.

Shuttle running

Six marks are put down at 5-metre intervals. Each individual is timed as he runs from the starting line to each line and back in turn commencing with the nearest. After each complete shuttle he has a fixed period of rest and repeats the activity six times. The total time taken is recorded. Professional footballers and international hockey players usually achieve figures between 180 and 200 seconds. Young players should aim to be no more than 10 seconds outside those figures.

Progression should be as in other exercises by reducing the initial rest period of 40 seconds by one second per week until a recovery period of 30 seconds is achieved. As individuals vary so widely an accurately kept training diary is really a necessity if each person is to obtain the maximum benefit from training.

Circuit training

Perhaps the best method of individual fitness training is circuit training. It can be undertaken in a daily period of time not exceeding half an hour and be performed at the player's home. When drawing up a circuit always ensure that exercise of a particular muscle group is always followed by one which utilizes a different group.

The circuit below requires no special equipment:

Burpees

Abdominal curls

Shuttle run

Wrist rolling

Step-ups

Split jumps

Back raise

Chins or single arm pull-ups

Press-ups

100 skips

Procedure

The player performs each activity for a maximum time of 45 seconds and a record is kept of his achievement. The totals are halved to set him a number of repetitions of each activity to perform in 30 seconds. He should move to each activity without pausing and complete two or three repetitions of the whole circuit, always starting at a different place.

Once the activities have been learned and the circuit completed within the required time, improvement can be obtained by increasing the number of the repetitions of each activity or reducing the time allowed.

Every player should remind himself that he must try to perform the activities in a good style. There is nothing to be gained by cheating or cutting corners.

The above suggestions should help to get players fit and other practices more directly related to cricket should now be introduced.

Sandpit or mattress catching

This exercise is best performed on sand or a thick mattress, gym mat, etc. Four catchers stand in a square about 3 to 4 paces apart and throw a ball to each other around the perimeter of the square. An interceptor kneels in the centre and tries to intercept each catch. This is very energetic, but a splendid exercise for wicket-keepers and others. Initially a minute at a time will be sufficient, though this can be extended as fitness increases.

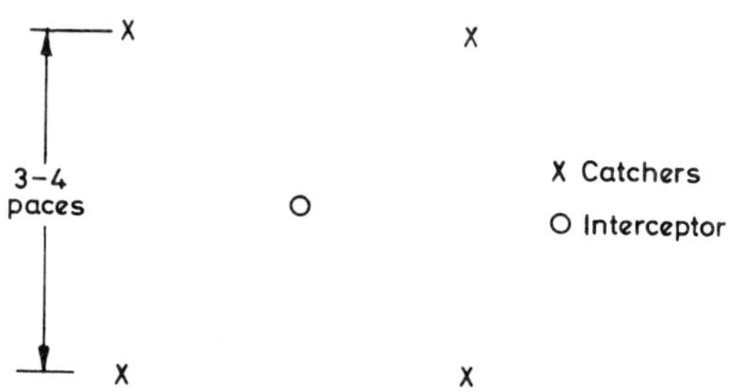

Shuttle retrieving

In this exercise the fielder sets off from a given point, runs to pick up a dead ball, turns and throws to a wicket-keeper before returning to the starting point. He does this six times against the clock. The distance to run can be increased progressively to provide a more difficult task, or the time allowed can be shortened.

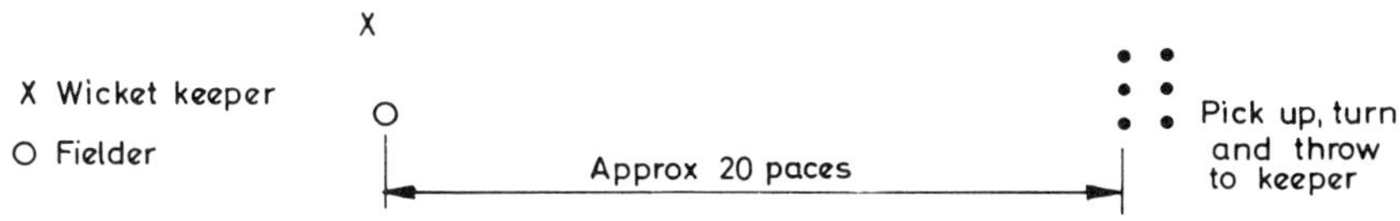

Shuttle catching

Two throwers stand about 15 metres apart with the wicket-keeper midway between them. A catcher stands about 15 metres in front of one of the throwers. The other thrower lobs the ball out in front of him so the catcher has to run to catch it. He then throws to the wicket-keeper. As soon as he has thrown it the other thrower throws his ball so that the catcher returns to his starting position to catch this ball. This is repeated six times against the clock and can be made harder by lengthening the distance to be run or decreasing the time allowed.

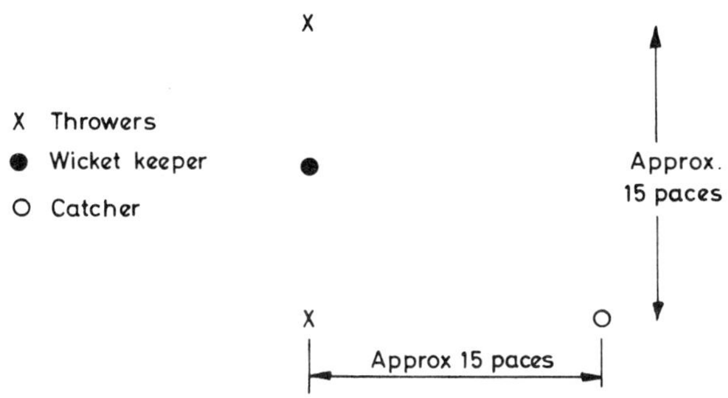

Ground fielding shuttle

In this exercise the fielder meets a ball coming straight at him. He moves in quickly, picks the ball up, flicks it underhand to the wicket-keeper and returns to his starting point to repeat the exercise six times against the clock.

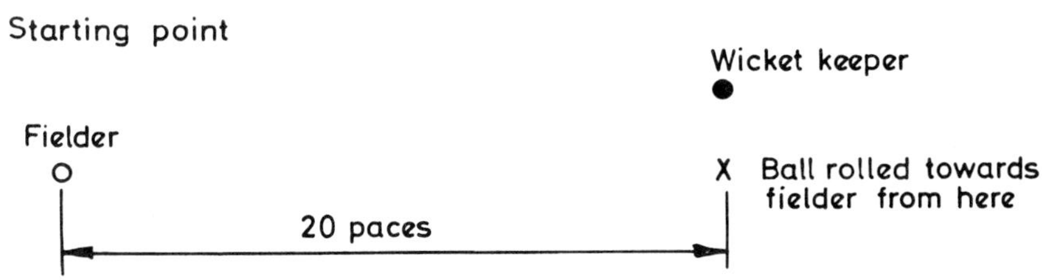

There are many variations of the above types of exercise and coaches will have their own favourites. However, fitness and skill training exercises are very different and though many exercises appear similar, the coach must bear in mind which is his prime object. Skills should be practised slowly and performed with the accent on the success of the skill required e.g. a successful catch, an accurate throw. Whereas the object of fitness training exercises is to complete the activity in as short a time as possible, **the success of fitness training exercises is measurable either in time taken, speed of recovery or work done** and not in the achievement of a large number of catches, etc. As fitness improves it becomes easier to perform skills in the game situation, since the player is more mentally alert and has sufficient energy to perform the task in the correct manner. Thus fitness training complements skill training in the development of good cricketers.

13

Grounds and Pitches

There are all too few cricket grounds in this country for those who want to play cricket, and on all too many of them the condition of the pitches and of the out-field is such as not only to detract from the pleasure of the players but also to make it very difficult for them really to learn the game.

The great batsman may triumph over a difficult pitch, the great fielder may, even on a rough ground, pick up cleanly most balls that come to him, but only too often the young cricketer can be fatally and finally discouraged by the conditions under which he plays. However much and however good the coaching he may get, he cannot be expected to 'keep his nose down' when batting if the length ball or even the half-volley may get up and hit him in the mouth, or to watch the ball until the last moment in ground fielding if the same thing may happen to him. If any coaching campaign is to bear as much fruit as it might, more and better grounds and, above all, more and better pitches, especially practice pitches, must be forthcoming.

The provision of new grounds and of the staff and equipment necessary for the proper maintenance of those that already exist is a matter for the public authorities, whether educational or municipal: so in the main is the problem of laying down artificial pitches, whether for match or practice. Of this nothing will be said here except to emphasize the immense value to the coach of even one such practice pitch with a really true playing surface as distinct from the rough and often dangerous turf wickets on which only too often he has to try to teach batting.

The object of this chapter is to offer some suggestions for the upkeep of grounds and the preparation of turf pitches. The resources both in equipment and in labour available will, of course, differ widely, though it is here suggested for official consideration that a generous outlay in equipment will not only make an immense difference to playing conditions but may well prove a profitable investment in the saving of labour-cost. Even where these resources are most meagre, it is hoped that much of the programme suggested will be found practicable and those who try to follow it can at least be sure that, however short of their aim the results of their efforts may fall, the boys who play on their grounds will have good cause to be grateful for them.

THE RECOVERY OF THE OUT-FIELD

In this section it is assumed that the out-field has been used for winter games. As soon as they are over and the weather permits, the following programme of culture should be carried out:

1. An application of inorganic nitrogen, i.e. nitro-chalk, or sulphate of ammonia, at the rate of approximately 35 grams per square metre (1 ounce per square yard). This helps to boost the growth of the existing grasses and also that of new grass as it germinates.
2. Scarify in all directions with a tilther rake or spike harrow.
3. Use a chain harrow, chain-link harrow or a drag brush to obtain an even surface and to form a tilth for newly sown seed. If a proprietary brush is not available then one can be improvised from wire-netting.
4. Aerate with a spiking machine to allow oxygen, light and moisture to enter the surface of the ground which may have been compacted by winter use.
5. Overseed with one of the following grasses – S23 or Stadion Melle. These are leafy perennial strains of Rye Grass which germinate quickly, withstand hard wear, and are drought resistant.

Take special care with the preparation and seeding of badly worn areas. Screened soil may have to be added to redress the levels, particularly in the goal areas. If possible, each goal mouth should be returfed, since turf will withstand the coming season's wear better than reseeded ground. Any areas which have become very heavily compacted can only be rejuvenated by harrow tining with a proprietary spiking machine. The subsequent cores of soil should not be removed, but once dry they may be broken up and scattered with a chain harrow. This process also forms an excellent tilth for reseeding. Spiking with a solid tined machine does not relieve compaction.

At this stage of the season far more harm can be done by rolling than by using no roller at all. The roller of a power mowing machine is usually adequate for the out-field.

For more detailed information consult the N.C.A. publication *Cricket – Take Care of Your Square.*

TREATMENT OF THE MATCH SQUARE AND NET PITCHES

(*a*) *Over which winter games have been played*

This problem arises when grounds are limited. It causes considerable problems but every effort must be made to help the ground to recover and to produce the best pitches possible for cricket.

The usual mistake made by inexperienced groundsmen is to use the heavy roller to flatten the surface. This should be avoided at all costs. Such an area requires a great deal of attention and initially the problem is to create sufficient new growth in the grasses. Early heavy rolling will compact the ground and inhibit growth.

1. Apply a dressing of nitro-chalk or sulphate of ammonia at the rate of approximately 35 grams per square metre (1 ounce per square yard).
2. Once the surface is reasonably dry, rake by hand to obtain an even surface and to form a tilth for reseeding. Add screened soil to ensure an even surface. This soil should be of medium texture, with a clay content. Use a lute to ensure an even distribution of the soil, so correcting any undulations.
3. Overseed with S23 Rye Grass at the rate of approximately 70 grams per square metre (2 ounces per square yard), working it into the tilth with a wooden rake. Although this type of grass is rather coarse it has many advantages. It germinates quickly, withstands hard wear, and with good cultivation forms a satisfactory sward for cricket.
4. After germination allow the new grass to grow to a height of approximately 40 to 50 millimetres ($1\frac{1}{2}$ to 2 inches), then mow to cut off the top 13 millimetres ($\frac{1}{2}$-inch). This should be repeated for the first four or five mowings. New grass should never be mown low, or it will die away.
5. As the grass becomes established it should be rolled with a light roller in two directions.
6. As the growth becomes stronger, so the mower can be set lower and the weight of the roller can be increased, until the area is ready for play.

During the dry period it is essential to keep such an area moist by artificial watering.

(*b*) *Over which no winter games have been played*

Renovation of the square must commence as early as possible after the conclusion of the cricket season. Any delay can be fatal.

1. Scarify to remove dead and decayed herbage and to open up the surface if it has become 'capped'.
2. Aerate by spiking. This operation is vital for the surface will have become compacted after rolling. A compacted surface excludes air, light and moisture and these are all essential for the production of a healthy sward.
3. Loosen the surface soil with a fork or rake, adding soil to correct the levels and then reseed any bare spots or areas with a thin growth. Care must be taken not to build up any areas with soil above the existing levels.
4. Returf the worn ends when the ground is sufficiently wet. Take care to lay the new turf to a true level.

5. Care for any new grass which germinates, treating any fungus disease at the first sign with a proprietary fungicide. Any weeds should be removed by hand. Selective weedkillers should not be used after mid-August. Mowing should continue until the growth of the grass ceases, taking care not to cut new grass too low.
6. When the new grasses have become established, aerate by spiking.
7. Top dress with a medium textured soil, screen, using a lute to ensure even distribution. No more than 3 millimetres ($\frac{1}{8}$-inch) new soil should remain on the surface. Continue to aerate periodically throughout the winter.

Spring preparation should commence as soon as the weather permits.

1. Roll lightly to even out the surface before taking the first cut with a mower which is set high.
2. As the surface becomes less moist increase the weight of the roller.
3. Gradually reduce the height of the cut, but never 'scalp' the surface, for grass gains its food through the foliage as well as the roots.
4. Feed with a balanced fertilizer during mid-April.

PREPARATION OF A MATCH PITCH

Preparation should commence some time before the pitch is required for use.

1. Select a site and mow a pitch 3 metres (10 feet) wide with a well-set machine. Give a double cut, both up and down the pitch.
2. Scarify lightly to thin out the grasses and to lift the grass to meet the mower blades. The surface soil must not be disturbed. If necessary, repeat this operation, for a grassy green pitch is not conducive to good cricket.
3. Mow several times, gradually reducing the cut to 3 millimetres ($\frac{1}{8}$-inch).
4. During dry weather water copiously with a sprinkler, or with a hosepipe and rose attachment. The water should penetrate to a depth of at least 50 to 75 millimetres (2 to 3 inches). Too little water is worse than no water at all.
5. When the surface is free from water and whilst the top 50 to 75 millimetres are still moist, commence to roll and continue until the necessary consolidation has taken place. Rolling should continue whilst there is any moisture in the top surface.
6. Throughout the period of preparation of a pitch it should be mown and brushed every other day until on the morning of the match it is brushed and mown very low, i.e. to 3 millimetres. This should be followed by a final rolling.

If possible, there should always be two or three pitches under preparation at any one time; each in a different stage of preparation.

14

Non-Turf Pitches

BACKGROUND

Throughout its long history, cricket in this country has traditionally been played on grass because the right soil and climatic conditions exist, and the skill to prepare good true turf pitches is available.

Today there are nearly 20,000 Cricket Clubs in Great Britain, and some 400,000 adult cricketers will be playing and enjoying their cricket on a fine summer afternoon in June.

The first positive indications for the need of artificial pitches were contained in the recommendations of the M.C.C. Cricket Enquiry Report of 1950 which urged the development of a suitable form of artificial pitch. At the suggestion of H.R.H. the Duke of Edinburgh, a Joint Committee consisting of representatives from M.C.C. and the National Playing Fields Association was set up to conduct research and trials.

Over the years the N.P.F.A. has provided the Secretariat and an advisory service to deal with any enquiries. A report was published and with the help of the L.C.C. many trials and experiments were undertaken in London parks. The work of the Joint Committee was phased out when the National Cricket Association took over the responsibility for the development of artificial pitches.

In 1973, with the backing of their Supporters' Association, the Warwickshire C.C.C. constructed eight practice non-turf pitches at the County Ground, Edgbaston, where trials of a wide range of materials have been conducted. Cricketers and Education Authorities have been invited to inspect these pitches and to play on them if they so wished.

There has, however, been a growing awareness amongst administrators and cricketers alike that there is still a declining standard in cricket pitches at the lower levels of the game. Recent surveys carried out by N.C.A. would support this view and there would appear to be several reasons for the decline:

1. The excessive usage of playing fields due to a shortage of land resources.
2. The limited durability of turf as compared with certain non-turf materials. For example, Astroturf for football has ten times the playing capacity of grass. Over-play on grass accelerates deterioration.
3. The high cost of labour, and the resulting lack of skilled groundsmen

to prepare and maintain good pitches. Many Local Education Authorities now use mobile labour units to maintain playing fields. But these do not adequately prepare cricket pitches which of course require specialized treatment.

4. The ever-increasing cost of materials and machinery required.
5. The lack of interest shown by P.E. staff in many schools. There is an urgent need for greater emphasis to be placed on cricket in the curricula of Colleges of Education; cricket should be given a share of the summer sunshine with other sports.

It is stressed that good pitches and coaching are synonymous. It is impossible to teach a child the basic skills of the game on a rough pitch where he might get hurt or frightened and therefore give up the game for some other activity. In this age of selectivity and competition from other sports and leisure pursuits, every effort should be made to anchor his loyalty to the game.

Apart from England, most cricketing countries use the non-turf pitch extensively except for the first-class game. In Australia, for instance, it is the concrete base with a coir or malthoid surface. In India and Pakistan, the coir or jute mat is used widely on grass or earth foundations. Canada, Holland, Denmark and Trinidad are countries where there are virtually no grass pitches; cricket is played on a hard porous water-bound base with a matting surface. Test Matches were being played on matting in some countries until recent years because it was expedient to do so.

Prejudice

It should be remembered that many countries are producing good cricketers who have been substantially brought up on non-turf pitches. Alas, however, there is in the U.K. a deep-rooted prejudice amongst cricketers against playing on a synthetic pitch. There are of course a number of reasons for this.

Traditionally cricket in this country has always been played on grass and there is a reluctance, particularly amongst leading players, to consider other forms of playing surface. The first-class game, which provides the shop window of cricket, has set the pattern for others to follow. There is the glorious uncertainty of the grass pitch which provides infinite variation in the game; it is said that if cricket is played on a non-turf pitch with standardized playing characteristics, it will produce a stereotyped player and a part of the excitement and entertainment value of the game will be lost. There is a lack of knowledge and a feeling that only low grades of cricket resort to non-turf pitches – they are thought to be more dangerous than turf.

It is a point for consideration, whether success at a game of skill such as cricket, should depend to such a large extent on the vagaries of the weather, and the uncertainty of the playing surface. No other sport, at international or any other level, leaves the outcome of the contest to such chance, where the playing conditions could be totally different for the two contesting teams.

The advantages

There are several factors which favour the use of a non-turf pitch, so perhaps these should be considered for a moment:

1. A turf pitch will only sustain a limited amount of play. In certain circumstances, therefore, such as in urban areas and at schools, there will always be the problem of preparing a good turf pitch, because the demand for use will far exceed the actual capacity of the turf table.
2. The non-turf pitch is much harder-wearing than grass, and could be used over and over again with the minimum of preparation. The groundsman is not dependent on maintaining a complete turf square, in order to meet the demands of cricket. A non-turf pitch will therefore take up much less space in a playing field, and can be sited to give the maximum use of the area.
3. The initial cost of construction may be relatively high, but once laid down, the non-turf pitch should need only limited preparation and maintenance as compared with turf. However, the importance of regular maintenance, where necessary, cannot be stressed too strongly.
4. A properly constructed non-turf pitch will always be true and level; its playing characteristics can be regulated, and these will remain constant – an important factor for coaching.
5. In wet weather, non-turf pitches will dry out much more quickly than turf, and less playing time will therefore be wasted. Furthermore, these are less vulnerable to vandalism.

STRUCTURE OF A PITCH

The laws of cricket are precise concerning the dimensions of the pitch and its markings. No mention is made, however, about its composition or the substance with which it should be made, although in the laws it is presumed to be grass. In Great Britain, turf has been the traditional playing surface, and it is stressed again that no real substitute for a good true fast turf pitch has yet been found; nevertheless there is today a compelling need for the greater use of the synthetic pitch.

In order to provide a non-turf pitch which is acceptable to cricketers there has to be a combination between the base and the playing surface, in order to provide satisfactory playing characteristics.

There are, of course, various materials in the market which have been used or are under trial.

In order to reach a fair assessment of the qualities of a non-turf pitch, it is necessary to consider its structure, which is made up as follows:

1. *Foundation*

The foundation or base upon which the 'playing surface' can be laid or fixed obviously should be smooth, hard and level. For outdoor use it is usually concrete (or moveable concrete units) or asphalt, requiring no maintenance. On the other hand, a hard porous waterbound base with a coir sisal mat, will provide an excellent pitch – but it needs constant maintenance; watering, brushing and rolling are essential for the base. The mat has to be pegged down, stretched periodically, and stored away after a match. Adequate labour is therefore needed.

Where a surface is to be fixed to a concrete base course, it is strongly recommended that a water-proof membrane such as polythene sheeting is inserted between the soil and the concrete base course, to prevent rising damp.

It should be borne in mind that the hard, porous, water-bound base, which is being used increasingly for outdoor play areas by other sports, forms only the base of the cricket pitch; a mat or some other material is required for the playing surface.

2. *Playing surface*

The ideal playing surface should assimilate as closely as possible the playing characteristics of a true, hard, turf pitch. These conditions are seldom attained in this country because of the climatic conditions except in the higher levels of the game.

The batsman should be given the opportunity of playing strokes in accordance with the accepted techniques of the game, and at the same time the bowler should have the chance of achieving success due to his skills rather than the vicissitudes of the pitch. The playing characteristics should therefore be judged by the pace, the bounce and the spin of the ball. They will, of course, vary depending on the combination of materials used for the foundation and the surface, but a balance between bat and ball should be the aim.

3. *Bowler's run-up*

All too often, the bowler's run-up and the area around the popping crease are neglected – the area which has to stand up to the greatest wear and tear. Further research has yet to be done in this connection, but there are one or two pointers to remember:

Firstly it is essential that footwear with steel spikes or studs should not be worn. Boots are available today with ripple soles, or with special nylon cleats, such as footballers wear. Cricketers should be encouraged to experiment with these, particularly in wet weather in order to establish their reactions when the pitch is slippery.

Secondly the pitch (i.e. the playing surface) should extend at least 1·22–4·88 metres (4–16 feet) beyond the stumps at each end, to enable the bowler to be on the surface in his delivery stride (*see* Fig. 1). For

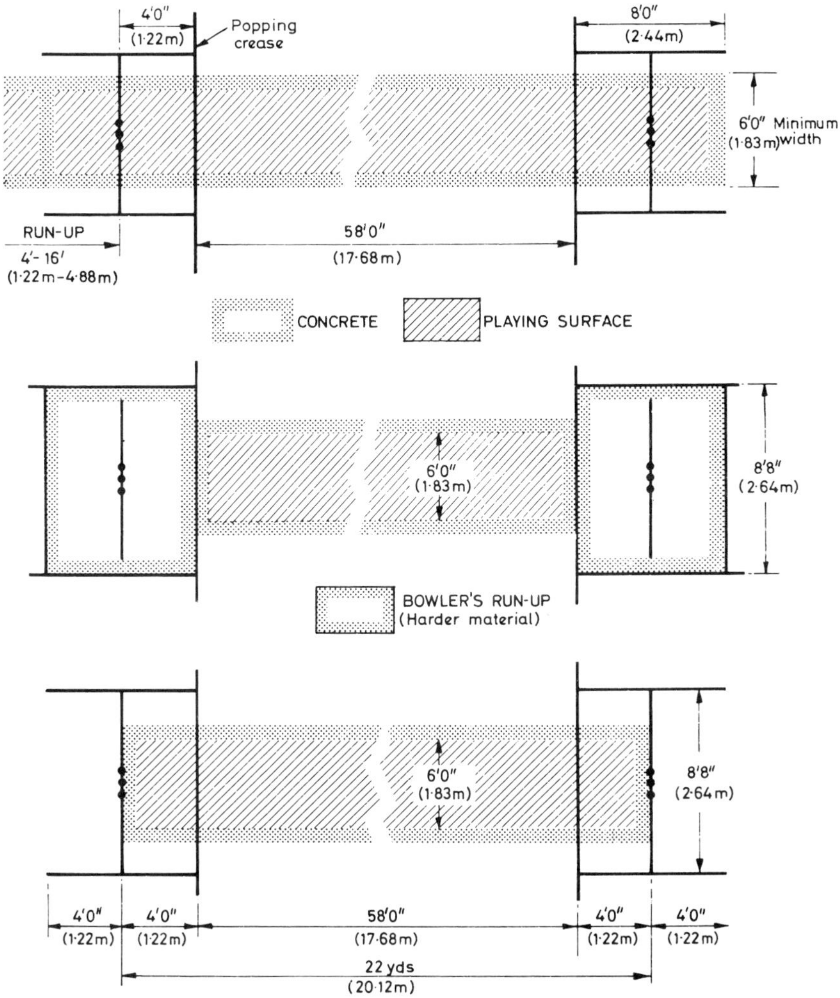

Fig. 1. The dimensions of a non-turf pitch

economy reasons, the matting or playing surface is usually only 20·12 metres (22 yards) long by 1·83 metres (6 feet) wide. This should be a minimum width: 2·44 metres (8 feet) is preferable.

CHOICE

There are on the market a number of materials which will provide a satisfactory playing surface, but unfortunately they may well vary from time to time due to a change in their specification or method of production, with a consequent variation in playing characteristics. The introduction of a 'Seal of Approval' would certainly help to overcome this difficulty. When considering the purchase of a synthetic pitch, it is important to ensure that the pitch of your choice has been tried out properly and has proved satisfactory to the cricketer. There are certain factors which should be borne in mind before making this choice:

1. The standard of cricket which is to be played on the pitch, e.g. schools, parks or clubs, and the age groups involved.
2. The financial resources available to meet the initial cost including the base.
3. The availability of labour and the extent to which preparation and maintenance will be required.
4. Vandalism and the extent to which the surface might suffer.
5. The flexibility of the product and the multi-purpose use to which it can be put as a playing surface.
6. Comfort to the user – the enjoyment of a game complements a player's skill.
7. Durability of the material, ease of repair and its safety factor, particularly in schools.

THE FUTURE

At the moment there is no magic carpet which will provide the 'pitch of perfection' for every occasion. The importance of quality of the product and the manufacturer's reliability to provide an after-sales service are stressed. The acid test is, of course, the user of the product; so an inspection and trial of the surface should be sought before a final choice is made.

It would seem that the non-turf pitch has a great potential for the future. There are prejudices to be overcome, money to be found for research and development, and there is a need for a greater awareness by school and Local Education Authorities of the importance of a good pitch for cricket.

The support and co-operation of first-class cricketers would be of immense value in the promotion of the non-turf pitch within the cricket scene. It is now accepted that the provision of better pitches will contribute in no small measure to the well-being of the game in a very competitive world of sport.

The challenge is there: cricket cannot afford to disregard it.

Anyone interested in the use of non-turf pitches should write to the National Cricket Association at Lord's Cricket Ground for the latest information on the subject and particularly in regard to suitable materials available on the market.

15

The Laws

During the last two hundred or more years the conduct of the game of cricket has been governed by a series of Codes of Laws. These Codes were at all times subject to additions and alterations laid down by the governing authorities of the time. Although there is little doubt that the game was subject to recognized rules as early as 1700, it was not until the formation of the Marylebone Cricket Club in 1787 that the Club has been recognized as the sole authority for the Laws, their interpretation and all subsequent alterations.

The various Codes produced over the years have, of course, shown changes – some great, some small – but on the whole the basic principles of the game have changed very little since the middle years of the nineteenth century, and the Laws have stood the test of time remarkably well. M.C.C. have, particularly in more recent times, consulted the cricket-playing countries of the world when changes in the Laws have seemed desirable, but they have steadfastly resisted the temptation to make a change for change's sake. They have, moreover, opposed the introduction of amendments merely to cover very rare incidents – sometimes purely hypothetical – in what is, after all, a complicated game and one which rests so much on the spirit in which it is played.

It is regrettable, but nevertheless true, that many players at all levels have only a superficial knowledge of the Laws. Although it may be unreasonable to expect them to acquire the detailed knowledge desirable for umpires, it is essential to the full enjoyment of the game that players have a sound understanding of the Laws, and, therefore, of the umpire's job. To achieve this, coaches should ensure that a knowledge of the Laws forms part of any coaching curriculum. Every endeavour should also be made to establish a good relationship between players and umpires with a mutual respect for one another.

Quite naturally, players expect the highest standard of umpiring, but, like all of us, umpires are not infallible and occasionally make mistakes. Seldom do these result from lack of knowledge, but rather of judgement. In the first-class game television playbacks not only highlight decisions for viewers, old and young, to interpret, but at times show players dissenting: such conduct on the field does immense harm to the spirit and well-being of the game.

Coaches must impress upon young cricketers the importance of the immediate acceptance of a decision, and the undesirability of putting undue strain on an umpire whose job is already difficult enough. The good example of the latter is the appealing for l.b.w. by fielders in positions from where it is quite impossible to assess the many considerations the umpire must apply before reaching his decision. Again, it is a question of a knowledge of the Laws – and the unworthy thought in some players' minds that the louder and more widespread the appeal the greater is the chance of getting a decision in their favour.

It must be appreciated by the players that the umpires are not 'enemies' but are there to ensure the fair conduct of the game.

During coaching sessions it should be possible to arrange discussions and 'quizzes' on the Laws – ample subject matter can be found in *Know The Game: The Laws of Cricket*, published on behalf of M.C.C., and from *Cricket Umpiring and Scoring*, the official textbook of the Association of Cricket Umpires. If young cricketers grow up with a knowledge of the Laws and an understanding of the umpire's problems, it will assuredly lead to the game being more enjoyable for all concerned.